From the Cross to Pentecost

FROM THE CROSS TO PENTECOST

God's Passionate Love for Us Revealed

T. D. JAKES

HOWARD BOOKS
A DIVISION OF SIMON & SCHUSTER, INC.

New York · Nashville · London · Toronto · Sydney

Howard Books
A Division of Simon & Schuster, Inc.
1230 Avenue of the Americas
New York, NY 10020

First Howard Books hardcover edition March 2010

For information about special discounts for bulk purchases,
please contact Simon & Schuster Special Sales at 1-866-506-1949
or business@simonandschuster.com.

The Simon & Schuster Speakers Bureau can bring authors to your
live event. For more information or to book an event contact the
Simon & Schuster Speakers Bureau at 1-866-248-3049 or visit our
website at www.simonspeakers.com.

Designed by Stephanie Walker

Manufactured in the United States of America

10 9 8 7 6 5 4 3 2 1

Library of Congress Cataloging-in-Publication data is available.

ISBN 978-1-4391-9480-5
ISBN 978-1-4391-9501-7 (ebook)

CONTENTS

FROM
THE CROSS
TO PENTECOST

OF MAN'S FIRST DISOBEDIENCE, AND
THE FRUIT
OF THAT FORBIDDEN TREE WHOSE
MORTAL TASTE
BROUGHT DEATH INTO THE WORLD,
AND ALL OUR WOE,
WITH LOSS OF EDEN, TILL ONE
GREATER MAN
RESTORE US, AND REGAIN THE
BLISSFUL SEAT
SING, HEAVENLY MUSE.

—*John Milton*

Chapter 1

ACCESS DENIED

I hear people ask the question over and over today: "What is the relevancy of the Cross of Jesus Christ? What does it matter to me that Christ died on a Cross over two thousand years ago? How does His Cross add any value to my life and to who I am and to who I want to be? What difference does it make whether Jesus rose from the dead? Even if He did, I'm going to go to work tomorrow just as I always have. It's not going to make any difference to me or to my family, or to my attitudes or my daily life. So why should I care about the so-called *Good News*?"

Perhaps it's a question you've asked yourself or someone else and never received an answer to that you considered to be satisfactory. If that's the case, I want to answer your question once and for all, but not in the way you might be expecting. I could tell you that the Cross of Christ is the hinge of all the world's history, and that it is without a shadow of a doubt the most crucial historical event that is the foundation for your relationship with God. We've created a holiday to acknowledge and celebrate the resurrection of Jesus—and I believe the foundation for this holiday to be true. But to start there is to try to present the solution before you understand the problem. If all you've heard is a list of what someone thought were solutions, it is very anticlimactic for me or anyone else to point first to the power of the Cross and the resurrection of Jesus until you are aware of the universal human dilemma—the degradation and the depravity of the human soul, which includes mine and yours and everyone else's—the answer is irrelevant.

Nobody searches for an answer if they don't have a question. No one seeks a solution if they're not convinced they have a problem. I know that was true in my life. Until I came to see what the true nature of my heart was like, the Cross just didn't make a lot of sense. But in the process of discovering who I really was, of seeing the real me, I found my soul crying out for answers.

So before I focus on the *consequences* of the Cross, I will shine a light on the *dilemma* that brought us to the point where we need the Cross in the first place.

Understand Who God Is

Comprehending why and how the Cross of Christ makes a difference in our lives starts with an understanding of who God is.

One of the first things we need to understand is that our God is eternal, He is an everlasting and dateless God—One who is without a beginning or an end of days. King David said, "From everlasting to everlasting, thou art God" (Psalm 90:2). He rules in eternity, which is timeless—there are no days, no weeks, no hours, no seconds. God simply exists in eternity.

Before God made man, the Bible says He formed the earth, and then through a divine process He began to fill the earth with good things. There is a life principle here that I don't want you to miss: Whenever God forms a thing, He will fill it. That is as true for your life today as it was in His original creation.

> Whenever God forms a thing, He will fill it.

You don't need to worry about filling your life, because whenever God forms something, He will fill it.

> He formed the earth and then filled it with abundant life.
> He formed the sea and then filled it with great whales and fish.
> He formed the open firmament and filled it with birds.
> He formed the dry land and filled it with grasses and trees.
> Finally, He formed man and breathed in him the breath of life so that he became a living soul, placing man in time.

The concept of *time* requires some stretching of your mind, but consider *time* as a sliver between two eternities— eternity future and eternity past. Thomas Carlyle said, "One life—a little gleam of time between two eternities." Man was placed in a sliver of time, just for a moment really, an interlude, an interruption between eternity future and eternity past.

If we can capture the thought of eternity in our minds, it will change . . .

> the way we view God,
> the way we view life,

the way we view ourselves,
the way we face problems,
and the way we deal with death.

If we begin to comprehend that all of the business and interaction we are experiencing in this present world is merely a brief interruption in an ongoing relation of eternity, our perspective on all of life will change. If we come to grips with the fact that we are eternal, and that we are going to live somewhere forever—though we may not be able to define *eternity* so as to satisfy a metaphysician—we will be amazed and transformed by the wonder of the meaning of life.

We don't have to be theologians to understand that we are eternal. Science informs us that all matter is eternal, and that it continues to exist in one form or another. It then corroborates what the Bible validates: "Before I formed thee in the belly I knew thee; and before thou camest forth out of the womb I sanctified thee, and I ordained thee a prophet unto the nations" (Jeremiah 1:5). That's what God told Jeremiah: "Before you even got here, I picked you out. I had predestined you. I had predetermined you. I prearranged for you to be who you are and where you are at this particular window of time."

That is not just true for the prophet Jeremiah. The same is true for you and me!

God is amazing! God is astounding! God is incredible! He is power and purpose. He is the fusion of energy and intellect. He is a strategist, and He has a plan for everything, including our lives. What I love about Him is not just that He is powerful—our God is a thinking God, a *logos* God, an intelligent God, and He has a plan. That gives me joy, because sometimes I don't have a plan; and when I do have a plan, oftentimes my plan goes awry. But it helps me understand that when my life seems chaotic and crazy, that God has a strategy for my life. According to Romans 8:28, I can rest assured that "All things work together for good to them that love God, to them who are the called according to his purpose."

You and I are called out of eternity into time according to His purpose and plan.

We must also understand that God is good and that He is sovereign. That means that God is in complete control, and that out of His goodness and His mercy, He chooses to be good because He is intrinsically good. There is no need for someone to police God or watch over Him. He just chooses to be good. And out of His goodness and sovereignty, God decided, as

Man is the crescendo of God's creation.

the final act of creation, to make man. Man, then, is the crescendo of His creation.

We must also understand that God is a loving God, and out of the incomprehensible depths of His love, He created someone to love. The greatest love story we will ever read is found between the books of Genesis and Revelation, because God handcrafted an object to love. In essence, He said, "I want something to love," and He took that something out of eternity and brought it down into time. He scooped up a bit of clay and began to form and fashion man into His likeness and into His image so that He might have someone to love.

If you believe that is true, you'll understand that we are far more interested in religion than God is. God is not interested in religion; He is interested in relationship. Religion only becomes significant when it enhances relationship, which it doesn't always do. Oftentimes religion becomes a deterrent to relationship. The Bible is filled with numerous religious people who missed connecting with God altogether. Sometimes we are so preoccupied with our religious ideologies and teachings and doctrines and principles, we fail to understand that what really matters the most in life is a relationship with God. It is from our foundational relationship with God that He gives us the privilege of having healthy relationships with our spouses, our families, our friends, and countless others.

It all starts with a relationship with God—that is the foundation for our lives that everything else must be built upon. If we try to build on any of these other relationships, we are building on quicksand, because at some point our relationship with our children will break down, our relationship with our siblings will break down, our relationship with our spouse will break down, and our relationship with our parents will break down. But our relationship with God is founded on a sure foundation, and we can deal with everything else once we stabilize that essential relationship.

"In the Beginning . . ."

Consider these opening words regarding creation from Genesis 1:1–8:

> *In the beginning God created the heaven and the earth. And the earth was without form, and void; and darkness was upon the face of the deep. And the Spirit of God moved upon the face of the waters.*
>
> *And God said, Let there be light: and there was light. And God saw the light, that it was good: and God divided the light from the darkness. And God called the light Day,*

and the darkness he called Night. And the evening and the morning were the first day.

And God said, Let there be a firmament in the midst of the waters, and let it divide the waters from the waters. And God made the firmament, and divided the waters which were under the firmament from the waters which were above the firmament: and it was so. And God called the firmament Heaven. And the evening and the morning were the second day.

Note that the Holy Spirit of God (see paragraph above) was present, even in creation. Open your Bible and read the rest of the creation account for yourself. Notice that each day God unfolded another facet of His strategy—from the second day to the third day to the fourth day there was the scattering of the stars into the skies, the releasing of the moon into the night, and the hurling of the sun into the atmosphere. Finally, after the vegetation had been created and the agricultural aspects of the creation had been resolved, He placed the cattle in particular regions to live and to graze. God provided for it all.

God did not create anything that had a need before first creating the provision. It's not as though God created schools of fish and then said, "Oops, I better create some water quick! Hold on! It's coming." It's not as though God created cattle and then said, "Hmmm, I wonder what they are going to eat?" When the panda bears arrived in creation, I'm sure He had bamboo shoots waiting, knowing they would love them.

Don't let this point escape your attention. If we have a need (and who doesn't?), it is only a sign there is a provision from the Creator to fulfill it. If we have a problem, God already has a solution. This has implications in all of our lives. For instance, "There hath no temptation taken you but such as is common to man: but God is faithful, who will not suffer you to be tempted above that ye are able; but will with the temptation also make a way to escape, that ye may be able to bear it" (1 Corinthians 10:13). God said it vividly through His creation, then He reinforces the same principle through the apostle Paul, saying, "I won't let you get into trouble without having a provision for any need." That's the kind of God He is!

Every detail of creation had to be considered and meticulously put into place, including the monitoring of the seasons so that each thing would cycle and reproduce after its own kind. There had to be the creating of seasons for each thing to have rest and recycling propensities. Everything had to be put in its place. The rocking of the oceans had to be controlled by the gravity that was controlled by the revolution of the sun and the earth moving around it, and all of it was put into a regimen of time. Every system was orchestrated and put in place so that the creation was finally a safe world into which He could put the object of His affection—mankind.

The Sixth Day

On the sixth day of creation, God stepped into the scene, scooped up some earth, and said, "Now, I'm going to start working on the beloved." "And the LORD God formed man of the dust of the ground, and breathed into his nostrils the breath of life; and man became a living soul" (Genesis 2:7). God breathed in man the "breath of *life*." Here the Greek translation of the Old Testament, the Septuagint, uses the Greek word *zoe* as the word for "life." God breathed into man "the breath of life" so that he became a living soul made in the image and likeness of the Creator (Genesis 1:27).

Adam woke up with everything he needed in place and available to him right there on the spot. And God said it was very good, because it *was* very good.

God had also created a honeymoon suite called the Garden of Eden (Genesis 2:8), and in it He placed the man and his bride, Eve, in a controlled environment that was so sustained that man was not required to do any hard labor at all. Adam was responsible "to dress [the Garden] and to keep it" (Genesis 2:15). All he had to do was love God, love his woman, and love his land. *All he had to do was love.* He didn't have to sweat. He didn't have to labor over deadlines. He didn't have to work around the clock. His job was to love and nurture. How sweet was that?

Women readers are now saying, "Hold on a minute. You left us out!" No, I didn't! You were in Adam. The first birth was actually a man giving birth. After Adam had walked around and named all the living creatures, we find that "for Adam there was not found an help meet for him" (v. 20). Adam looked at the giraffes and camels and said, "Those won't do." He looked at the crocodile and said, "No, not even close to what I'm looking for." He looked at the spider and said, "Too small." He looked at the cheetah and said, "Too fast." Finally, Adam said, "God, I'm not happy because I don't have what You have. You have something to love, and I don't. You created me so much like You, and I am made to love something in

> *Women readers are now saying, "Hold on a minute. You left us out!" No, I didn't! You were in Adam.*

relationship to me even as You have expressed Your love in my relationship to You."

And so it was that God "caused a deep sleep to fall upon Adam, and he slept," because God does His best work when we go to sleep. Then He reached inside Adam and "took one of his ribs, and closed up the flesh instead thereof; and the rib, which the LORD God had taken from man, made he a woman" (vv. 21–22). Essentially, God pulled Eve out from him. So women did not have the first C-section—Adam did!

Adam woke up, saw the woman, and said, "Whoa, man! What's up, Lord? She's cool!" God is good all the time, and Adam knew it. Look a little deeper at Adam's response to Eve: "This is now bone of my bones, and flesh of my flesh: she shall be called Woman, because she was taken out of Man" (v. 23). And Adam began to walk with the woman in the Garden, in their honeymoon suite, picking fruit whenever they were hungry, scooping water whenever they were thirsty, never having to worry about replenishing or recycling, because God put a perfect system in place.

How many years Adam and Eve lived in the Garden, enjoying each other and caring for the Garden, enjoying a relationship with God and learning about the creation, we do not know. The brief creation account only tells us what we need to know. But there is no reason to think it was a short time. We do know that the innocence of Adam and Eve extended into the years of fellowship in the Garden.

The Tree of the Knowledge of Good and Evil

I woke up one morning and noticed my watch had stopped in the night. I kept trying to wind it, but it wouldn't start. So I said to a friend, "My expensive watch won't work. See if you can fix it. I'm not that bright." He looked at it and said, "The battery must be dead." I said, "Duh!" Such an amazing technological mechanism is stopped by the lack of power. The whole system is completely shut down by a breach. The watch was useless to me in its condition of having lost its power.

On a far more profound level, we see something similar to this in Genesis 3: *The complete loss of power through a break in mankind's relationship with God.* This breakdown began with the choice of whether or not man would love God and obey His word. Alone in all of creation, man was faced with the call to a moral decision. Man was created as a free moral being who is given the power of deciding for himself. In placing Adam in the Garden, God established one crystal clear rule: "Of every tree of the Garden thou mayest freely eat: But of the tree of the knowledge of good and evil, thou shalt not eat of it: for in the day that thou eatest thereof thou shalt surely die" (Genesis 2:16–17). This tree symbolized all moral knowledge, knowledge that only God's power could sustain, and thus its fruit was forbidden to man.

The tree of life, on the other hand, was similar to a fully charged battery in the watch—it keeps the system going. As "the tree of life," it gives *life*, and by that I mean *eternal life*. It's an Eveready battery that will never lose its power—it continues to maintain the system. Isn't it interesting that God did not create anything that did not maintain the system? By that I mean, when was the last time the sun needed to be recharged, having burned up all the gas and run out of power? When did the world slow down on its axis so it could take a break, or when has the ocean ever said, "I'm tired. I don't think I will sway today. Call me tomorrow and perhaps I'll feel up to it again"?

Even our bodies were made to be eternal. For instance, the moment I cut my finger, white blood corpuscles rush to that cut to stitch my body back together, because my body was not originally designed to die.

The tree of life is the battery that perpetuates the motion—tick, tick, tick, tick, tick—and the whole creation system operates around the tree of life. Every facet of creation was good, very good. Adam enjoyed it and explored it and loved it. There was pure joy and peace, and God rested from His labors. Whenever we see God sit down, we know it is done and all is well.

God loves when we come to Him as children and simply do what He says without reasoning it all out, without over-processing the whys and the hows. There is something that God blesses in the midst of naïveté that is irreplaceable. It's one of the conditions of living in His Kingdom. Jesus said, "Except ye . . . become as little children, ye shall not enter into the kingdom of heaven" (Matthew 18:3). The problem is that some of us cannot really get hooked up with God because we overthink everything and don't just do what He says when He says. It's a lack of naïveté, a lack of childlike dependency, and a lack of vulnerability that stop us from having an intimate relationship with God, because we worship our minds and not God himself. We become like my watch that stopped because it was cut off from the sustaining power, and the system was broken.

There are two trees that God described within the Garden. One is the tree of the knowledge of good and evil, which will dispel the naïveté, the vulnerability, and the innocence. If the innocence is gone, what emerges is an independence that will stop us from having a deep relationship with another, because relationship requires the vulnerability of need, and independence denies that we have a need. If you've ever tried to have a relationship with someone who doesn't need you, you know how hard that is.

Consequently, once the recipient of God's love chose to trade places and wanted to forgo the love of God and run ahead of His loving guidance, and wanted to know, even as God knows, that innocence was shattered and the need was gone. And God said, "I've got to make some changes."

Take a good look at the nature of this tree of the knowledge of good and evil. Clearly, it was in the midst of the Garden to prove man's love. It was the one and only tree from which he could not eat. Love is only proven where choice exists. If there is no choice, there can be no genuine proof of love. For instance, if there

Love is only proven where choice exists.

is only one woman in the entire world and I say to her, "I love you above all others," it means nothing, because there is no other option. There is no reason for that woman to feel flattered, special, blessed, or excited when she knows she is the only one available.

The same is true for our lives. God has forbidden us some things so we can choose to obey Him, because our obedience validates our love. As the tree of the knowledge of good and evil was to Adam and Eve, the purpose of that "something" puts us into a system so that every day we can say, "God, see how much I love You? I have kept this rule because I would rather choose You above anything else in life." It is that preference that is at the heart of a relationship with God.

The Tempter Slithers In

But while Adam enjoyed the creation and God rested, a slithering thing wiggled its way into the Garden—a slinking, crawling, creeping thing that the Bible uses as an icon of evil. Understand that the serpent as the icon is not the issue—it is what the serpent is symbolic of—evil—that is significant. When you touch it, it opens up hell's kitchen.

The serpent naturally focused on the tree of the knowledge of good and evil, knowing that it was the key to breaking man's relationship with God. Coming to Eve alone, he said, "Ye shall not surely die: For God doth know that in the day ye eat thereof, then your eyes shall be opened, and ye shall be as gods, knowing good and evil" (Genesis 3:4–5). In essence, the serpent was saying that God was withholding something good from her and would be jealous and envious if she took it, because then she would be like Him. The serpent planted the seed in Eve's mind that God was afraid that if they ate of the fruit of the tree of the knowledge of good and evil, they would know even as He knows, and then they would be like Him. "That's why God made the rule. He's keeping you from becoming gods yourselves!"

Curiosity was aroused by the temptation. Eve stopped and looked. She reflected and talked when she should have fled the scene. Such a beguiling argument! Undoubtedly, Eve had never thought such a thought. The serpent played upon Eve's desire to be like God, twisted it around, and got her to question why the rule was there in the first place. Surely it is a good thing to become like God. It's the same thing we want today—to become like Jesus Christ. But Eve went about a right thing in a wrong way. The oldest trick in the world is to get us to do the right thing in the wrong way.

It's amazing how the enemy still uses the same tricks on us over and over again. He even tried it in the temptation of Jesus during the forty days in the wilderness. In Matthew 4, the Bible states that after Jesus had fasted forty days and forty nights, He was hungry, and it was right for Him to eat. But "when the tempter came to him, he said, If thou be the Son of God, command that these stones be made bread" (Matthew 4:3). The fast had ended, and it was not wrong for Jesus to eat, but in this situation it would have been wrong for Jesus to use divine power to accomplish this human need. Satan tempted Jesus to go about doing the right thing in the wrong way. But instead of falling prey to the lie that Eve believed, and that we often believe, Jesus hit the devil with the Word of God and drove him away: "It is written, Man shall not live by bread alone, but by every word that proceedeth out of the mouth of God" (v. 4).

All temptations play upon trying to satisfy legitimate needs in illegitimate ways. So we are not wrong to have the need, but we may be wrong with the method we employ to accomplish the need.

First the Woman, Then the Man

Once Eve had been deceived into believing the enemy's lie, she reached out after the forbidden fruit—whether it was an apple, an orange, or a tangerine doesn't matter, because it was what it represents that matters. In that moment, her eyes were opened, and the results were far different from what she or Adam would have expected. Instead of gaining superior knowledge that made them equal with God, they gained an overwhelming awareness of guilt and shame.

You see the impact that followed. Eve immediately reversed the divine order of their marriage. Rather than Eve being the recipient of the provision, she became Adam's provider and gave to the man rather than the man giving to her. "She took of the fruit . . . and gave also unto her husband with her; and he did eat" (Genesis 3:6).

However, it wasn't Eve's eating of the forbidden fruit that brought the world down, so we need to stop blaming women for The Fall. Eve innocently fell prey and was deceived, but Adam knew exactly what he was doing as she gave it to him and he ate. This problem falls squarely on Adam's shoulders. He consciously made the decision, for God had told him specifically that "in the day that thou eatest thereof thou shalt surely die" (Genesis 2:17).

I think that Adam looked at the situation and made the decision that if Eve was going to die, he would die with her in disobedience rather than obey God. We see in Adam a type of Christ. He was the "first Adam" (1 Corinthians 15). Both the first Adam and the last Adam—who was Christ—had the same dilemma. The last Adam's bride—the Church—

was dying, too. If He had disobeyed the Father, He would have taken the bait of the first Adam, and He would have died with His bride. But instead of dying with His bride, *Jesus Christ died for His bride and broke the curse.* Jesus reconnected the battery—tick, tick, tick, tick—and redemption started.

> *Instead of dying with His bride,* Jesus Christ died for His bride and broke the curse.

With the juice of the fruit in their mouths, Adam and Eve looked at each other, and all their innocence was gone. Suddenly they knew that they were naked, and they were ashamed. In that historical moment in the third chapter of Genesis, we see the phenomenal crash of mankind. Like a magnificent airplane falling out of the clear blue sky and crashing into the deepest ocean, mankind plummeted down into the depths of depravity so low that The Fall has not stopped yet. It continues to plummet downward until every baby is born in sin and shaped in iniquity. There is no need for classes that teach us how to sin—it is inherent from The Fall. No one teaches a two-year-old child how to lie about sneaking a cookie—it's inherent from Adam.

"Adam, Where Art Thou?"

God walked through the cool of the Garden and called out to Adam, "Where art thou?" (Genesis 3:9). This is a rhetorical question. God obviously knew the answer when He asked the question. God asked this to teach Adam as well as you and me a lesson, because one of the hardest things in life for a man to be honest about is where he is. We men fill our lives with work and career and money and toys and busyness to avoid having to answer the question: "Where am I?"

What the woman wants to know is, "Where are you?"

What the kids want to know is, "Where are you?"

What God wants to know is, "Where are you?"

And the truth is that most of us men honestly don't know where we are. We are lost—plain and simple. Not knowing where you are means you are lost.

Adam didn't answer, because he did not know the answer to "Where art thou?" The best he could have done was to respond, "God, I'm not sure." Most men can empathize with Adam. We know what it means to lose our ability to articulate where we are. If God asked us the same question, how would we respond other than to answer, "God, I'm lost! I don't know where I am."

By the way, God was never lost. We may say we "found the Lord," but I beg to differ with that statement. We didn't find God, because God wasn't lost. God is never lost. "The word is nigh thee, even in thy mouth" (Romans 10:8). God is in our next breath. He is in our prayer life. He is never lost. He is in our home. He is close to us. It's not God who is lost; it is us.

The Bible states that Adam's response was, "I heard thy voice in the Garden, and I was afraid, because I was naked; and I hid myself" (Genesis 3:10). As foolish as it was, Adam hid from God, which is exactly what we're still doing today. We would be shocked at how many people get up on Sunday morning, take a shower, go to great lengths and costs so they can look good to everyone in church,

> *As foolish as it was, Adam hid from God, which is exactly what we're still doing today.*

but all of it is a façade they're hiding behind. The real person is hiding beneath the well-groomed hair and the fancy clothes and the matching shoes. People only hide when they are afraid, and the voice of God is frightening when there is disobedience in our lives.

By way of contrast, "There is no fear *in love*; but perfect love casteth out fear" (1 John 4:18; emphasis mine). But where there is fear, we are always hiding. After all, who wants to be rejected and judged? Who wants to be exposed and seen for who they really are? The overwhelming fear of rejection makes both men and women hide.

The Big Cover-up

God found Adam and Eve hiding in the Garden, and what did He discover? "They sewed fig leaves together, and made themselves aprons" (Genesis 3:7). In their attempt to cover their nakedness and shame, they had gone and found a bush, cut off some leaves, and made themselves little aprons. Adam didn't realize that when he cut off the leaves, the same thing that was happening to the leaves was happening to him. The leaves were healthy and vital until he severed them from the life source. Adam and Eve were fine until they cut themselves off from God. Even though the leaves appeared green at that moment, even as they were weaving them together into aprons, the leaves were dying.

Even though a man looks good today, he is dying because he has cut himself off from God. This is always what happens when man tries to cover himself. That's what religion does—it covers us with works. We actually begin to think

God will accept us because we've done good things. We're saved *because* . . . anytime we have a "because," we have a religion. And anytime we have religion, it is blocking relationship. Nevertheless, we prop up leaves, man-made good deeds, hand-cut stuff that is withering and will eventually crumble, and soon we'll have to find something to replace it. An apron of leaves is a poor replacement for a lost relationship with God.

Understand that the aprons of leaves were withering even while Adam and Eve were stitching them up. The man and woman came out in the open before God and probably hoped they were acceptable to God. Adam presented to God what he'd made, but God did not accept it, although He did introduce Adam and Eve to what His Son Jesus would accomplish much later. God took animal skins and covered their nakedness (Genesis 3:21), because "without shedding of blood is no remission" (Hebrews 9:22).

Why is that true? Because God said, "But of the tree of the knowledge of good and evil, thou shalt not eat of it: for in the day that thou eatest thereof thou shalt surely die." What God introduced to mankind is the principle called *substitution*. If there is no death, then God is a liar; and if God is a liar, then Satan takes over. Something had to die so that

Adam could live, and that happened through the life of the innocent animal that died in his stead.

Consider the animal that gave up its skin to cover the man and woman. If it could talk, it would say, "No, no! Don't kill me! I didn't do anything wrong!" And God would have said, "That is exactly why I will take your life, because what I need is your innocence. Adam lost his innocence, and I'm going to take your innocence and give it to him. I'm going to take the guilt that Adam incurred, and I'm going to place it on your account so that the death you died is not in your name but in Adam's name, and the life that he lives is not in his name but in your name."

All of this is a temporary solution to a far bigger problem. This is merely a Band-Aid that is placed over a cancer, so it temporarily stops the oozing. But it doesn't heal the cancer. If the blood of bulls and goats could have healed the cancer of sin, Christ would not have had to die. But it would stop the oozing long enough so that man could live out his life, which he did. Otherwise he would have immediately died physically.

God Intervenes

With mankind lost and already free-falling into depravity, all of God's creation also fell into peril, and it's still in peril today, waiting on the manifestation of the sons of God (Romans 8:21). Looking around the world, we see that we are still falling downward. We ruin our water supplies, our lakes, our streams, our air, our oil, and other natural resources. Everything that God created for us, we are now destroying, because it is all part of the meteoric Fall of all mankind as we continue to live independent of the will and the purpose of God.

All that God had created seemed lost. The angels were aghast. There was no record that this had ever happened before. All that God labored over had now been placed in jeopardy—it was taken to the marketplace, it was auctioned off, and it was hocked. Later we will find that where it has been hocked by the first man, Adam, it must be redeemed by the second Adam, Jesus Christ.

> Everything was spiraling down.
> There was a gulf between God and man.
> They now knew sorrow and hard toil.
> Nature, once man's ally, had become hostile.

War broke out between the man and the woman.
Crisis broke out between their children until one
    murdered the other.
It was all spiraling down.

The Garden of Eden was lost, mankind was lost, but God was not finished with mankind. He said, "Wait a minute! I've got to deal with Satan: 'Thou art cursed above all cattle, and above every beast of the field; upon thy belly shalt thou go, and dust shalt thou eat all the days of thy life.' I've got to deal with the woman: 'I will greatly multiply thy sorrow and thy conception; in sorrow thou shalt bring forth children; and thy desire shall be to thy husband, and he shall rule over thee.' I've got to deal with man: 'In the sweat of thy face shalt thou eat bread, till thou return unto the ground' " (see Genesis 3:14–19).

God stepped in and dealt with each participant in The Fall, but another problem remained. The system was still working—tick, tick, tick, tick—because the tree of life was still there. And if God didn't do something about that, man would be eternally fallen, because the tree of life was still sustaining everything.

So God sent down cherubims from heaven and said to Adam and Eve, "I am going to drive you out of your honeymoon suite that I built for lovers to dwell in, and I am going to send you out into the world. You're going to be in the world, but not of it. You came from here, and you're going there. I'm placing my cherubim with a flaming sword that turns every way, and it will block the way back to the tree of life, because if man was to get to the tree of life in his fallen state, he would be eternally damned" (see Genesis 3:24). The reason God blocked the way to the tree of life was so that man cannot get to life, and the further he gets away from the tree, the more his knees hurt as he ages, the more his back goes out and his hair thins.

The tree of life is still giving life, but mankind cannot get to it anymore. It still has all the power it ever had, but man cannot reach it. Every time man would try to reach for its fruit, the flaming sword would stop him from having access. So mankind begins the slow, dangerous process of trying to find a way to eternal life without getting killed by the sword.

> The Flood came, and he couldn't find his way to eternal life.
> The Pentateuch came, and he couldn't do it.
> The goats died, and he couldn't do it.
> The lambs cried, and he couldn't do it.
> The incense went up, and he couldn't do it.
> The tabernacle came, and he couldn't do it.

The temple was built, and he couldn't do it.
The prophets came, and he couldn't do it.

But one day, this man Jesus came. He was born of a virgin, wrapped in swaddling clothes, and laid in a manger. When He grew, He walked among men, healed the sick, raised the dead, and turned water into wine. They tried to get Him to seek an office so they could make Him king over the earth, but He said, "My kingdom is not of this world" (John 18:36). And when the time was right, they drove nails into His hands and feet, and they pierced His side, because the only thing that could stop the flaming sword was the Cross of Christ.

That's why when I think of the goodness of Jesus and all of His love for me, my soul cries out, "Hallelujah! Now I can come to the Father boldly and obtain my Savior and find grace to help in the time of need. I come to the tree of life and receive the eternal life Jesus won for me!"

Oh Happy Day!

Two thousand years ago, Jesus Christ, the Lover of my soul, knew I was broken, knew I was fallen and couldn't get up, so He came for me. He knew I couldn't come to Him. He knew that it was no good for my mother to say to me, "Why don't you do better, honey?" He knew it was futile for my father to say, "Why don't you change your life, son?" Jesus understood that neither you nor I could come to Him because we were broken. But if we would just cry out to Him, He would come to us.

One Tuesday night in a tiny little church that was so small you couldn't even whip a cat in it, God found me. I was lost. Many times I had tried to come to Him. I couldn't do it. I couldn't make it. I couldn't reach high enough. Why? Because I was broken. But when I couldn't come to Him, Jesus came to me, and He saved me.

Today we have excellent programs available, from counseling programs to rehabilitation programs. We have systems in place that are supposed to help us, but they hold no real power. For God is saying, "Verily, verily I say unto you, with your rich self, with your broken self, with your attractive self, with your homely self, with your healthy self, with your afflicted self, you must be born again."

You can come shake my hand until my fingers fall off, but unless you give your heart to God, it will not make a difference.

"Adam, where art thou?"

He is still calling you today.
And nothing that you own,
and no matter where you live
or what you buy
or whom you have slept with,
have stopped that call.

If you'll listen for a moment,
that call is still coming
from the Savior's bleeding side
on Calvary's Cross.

"And, where art thou?"

WHEN I CONSIDER THY HEAVENS,
THE WORK OF THY FINGERS,
THE MOON AND THE STARS,
WHICH THOU HAST ORDAINED;
WHAT IS MAN, THAT THOU ART
MINDFUL OF HIM? AND THE SON
OF MAN, THAT THOU VISITEST
HIM? FOR THOU HAST MADE
HIM A LITTLE LOWER THAN THE
ANGELS, AND HAST CROWNED
HIM WITH GLORY AND HONOUR.

Psalm 8:3–5

Chapter 2

ACCESS GRANTED

Several years ago I heard a line from a movie that has stayed with me. The main couple in the movie was debating what sort of relationship they actually had. The question posed was, "How can we live together when we are so different?" The woman looked at the man, who had just declared his love for her, and she replied, *"A bird and a fish can fall in love, but where would they live?"* That's a profound way of asking what Tina Turner sang so famously, "What's love got to do with it?" The implication facing this couple was what to do when two entities from two widely different perspectives love each other. The issue becomes, "How do the two of us live together? How can we be together when you need something that I don't need, and I need something you don't? The fish lives in a reality that the bird would drown in—the bird breathes something that would choke the fish. I'm a bird, and you're a fish; so how do we make love work?"

This couple's predicament struck me as similar to the predicament that led Jesus Christ to the Cross of Calvary, for as I've already described, the first three chapters of Genesis show the love crisis between God and mankind coming to a head. You will never understand what I am saying as long as you perceive God as firmly seated in the bulwarks of heaven, mindful of mankind's Fall, of course, but not caring about it. You will never understand this grand love story until you recognize that our God is a passionate God. He is not a sovereign majesty who sits on a throne and executes judgments without feeling or compassion. If we did not have a God who is passionately interested in us, none of us would be here.

We will never truly appreciate the dynamics of who God is and what He has done in our lives, until we do recognize that the Cross and all God did that preceded it are one big, amazing, unbelievable love story. It is all about a God who fell in love with man, about Holiness falling in love with humanity, about the Celestial touching the terrestrial, and about the Majestic touching the mundane.

It is a shame that more people have not been taught about the wonder of the love of God. The apostle Paul's prayer for the Ephesian believers was that they "may be able to comprehend with all saints what is the breadth, and length, and depth, and height; and to know the love of Christ, which passeth knowledge, that ye might be filled with all the fulness of God" (Ephesians 3:18–19). Paul was saying, "I want you to know something that you cannot even know, because your finite little mind will never be able to grasp

> *You will never understand this amazing, unbelievable love story until you recognize that our God is a passionate God.*

the height, the depth, the breadth, the length—you will never find a measurement by which to measure how much God loves you!"

The Searing Pain of Separation

I've asked myself a thousand times: "How can God possibly love a person like me? Knowing all the wretchedness of my life, knowing all my failures and sins, whatever could possess Him to even think about me? Surely He can't stand me."

This is the situation we are considering in Genesis 3. We are looking at a God who carefully and succinctly laid up a love cottage called Earth and a boudoir called the Garden of Eden, then set a man and a woman in a controlled environment in which He might express His love. Yet from this height, this great majestic height of celestial love, man plummeted into the abyss and the atrocity of human depravity, substituting lust for love. He forfeited the opportunity to have eternal bliss in a relationship with God to spend a few moments in depravity with something in the flesh.

I want to take you back to the concluding passages of Genesis 3, because it is the end of utopia, the end of a spiritual, blissful idea that God had of living throughout eternity with the object of His affection, which was mankind, and it ended in despair. "And the LORD God said, Behold, the man is become as one of us, to know good and evil: and now, lest he put forth his hand, and take also of the tree of life, and eat, and live for ever: Therefore the LORD God sent him forth from the Garden of Eden, to till the ground from whence he was taken. So he drove out the man; and he placed at the east of the Garden of Eden Cherubims, and a flaming sword which turned every way, to keep the way of the tree of life" (vv. 22–24).

Reflecting on those verses, have you ever had a good relationship go bad? Have you ever invested passion and intensity and enthusiasm and creativity in someone who failed to reciprocate it? Have you ever loved someone with all your soul who turned you away for another lover? Then you know the grief that emerges from the lover's heart when love is not reciprocated. The mourning it produces is often even greater than the mourning we experience upon the death of someone who loved us while they lived. The death of a romantic heart is so painful, bleeding, glaring, and degrading that it often requires therapy to overcome the sense of rejection.

That represents something of the heart of God as expressed in Genesis 3, because now we see the divorce papers being finalized as God disannuls the relationship He had with humanity and as the man and woman sort out memories of a lost opportunity.

> Gone are the fellowship and the intermingling of the divine and the human.
> Gone are all the intricacies of the intimacies between God and the object of His affection.
> Gone is the Garden of Eden that God so meticulously orchestrated with streams and rivers to enrich it, and gone is the provision that they would live there forever.
> Gone are the delight and intimacy of love.
> Gone are the praises and worship that should have erupted from the human heart.

Gone is the passion that should have existed in the
    eye of His adoration.
Gone in one sweeping moment—all gone to hell.

The rejected God looked at the fallen man and woman, and in the anger that is only known by a rejected lover, He said, "Get out!" We can only get that angry when we have loved that much. Out of the depths of pain that Adam's rejection produced in the heart of God, He commanded Adam, "Get out of the Garden! Take Eve, take your stuff, and get out!" That was what was happening here.

Cut Off from the Tree of Life

The divorce seemed to be final, the decree had been written, and God drove the man and woman from the Garden. He had spoken; "Oh, you want to get near the tree of life and live forever? No, that is one of the benefits of loving Me. If you reject Me, you reject one of the benefits of living here. Go!"

With the haste of the guilty, Adam took his wife, Eve, and they began to move out of the divine favor of God into the perplexities of human existence. They turned their backs on the divine to walk into the human, never to have the melodious experience that the hymnist describes: "I come to the garden alone while the dew is still on the roses, and the voice I hear falling on my ear the Son of God discloses. And He walks with me and He talks with me and He tells me I am His own, and the joy we share as we tarry there none other has ever known."

Gone was the opportunity to hear the voice of the Lord walking through the cool of the Garden. Gone was the daily communion between them and God, which was so intricate that most theologians believe there was no blockage between heaven and earth—that man could look up into the very throne of God, and God could look down into the heart of humanity.

When God had called out, "Where art thou?" He found His beloved in the arms of the serpent, Satan. The betrayal was too much for the relationship to sustain, for when we move positionally, we also move conditionally. Thus, the divine Lawyer signed the paper, the creed was released, the love affair broke down, and they were no longer on speaking terms.

Adam and Eve, ashamed to look back, walked away from eternal life to eternal loss, trying to fill the void that love left with things that do not satisfy. And

> *Adam and Eve, ashamed to look back, walked away from eternal life to eternal loss, trying to fill the void that love left with things that do not satisfy.*

we're still trying to fill that same void, to our own destruction.

God's Disappointment

Imagine with me that at this point the Almighty God felt the way we would feel when love has gone bad. We feel disappointed and distressed.

There are few things that are foreign to God, because in His omniscience He knows all things—He knows the end from the beginning, and He knew us before He formed us in our mothers' bellies. But the Bible states repeatedly that there is something that God didn't know—He knew no sin. So Adam fell into something for which God had no point of reference. "Adam, where art thou? You just did something I've never done, and you've fallen into something I've never sat in, gone where I've never been. I love you, and I want to be reunited."

If you read from the book of Genesis through the book of Revelation, God unravels the plan that worked things out between Himself and man. This is the Bible—God's diary, filled with notes and plans and perspectives of working it out.

> The man had fallen into a sinful place where God could not live.
> God lives in a holy place where man cannot come.

The bird and the fish fell in love, but where will they
live?

Starting Over

God's first major step toward restoring His relationship
with mankind began with the man Abraham. He told Abraham to follow Him out of his home country and "I will es-
tablish my covenant between me and thee and thy seed after
thee in their generations for an everlasting covenant, to be
a God unto thee, and to thy seed after thee. And I will give
unto thee, and to thy seed after thee, the land wherein thou
art a stranger, all the land of Canaan, for an everlasting pos-
session; and I will be their God" (Genesis 17:7–8).

In essence, God said, "Abraham, I'm going to start this
thing over with you. I'm going to produce a seed in your body,
and this seed is the beginning." But it didn't work out the
way Abraham and Sarah thought it would. God waited until
Abraham's body was ninety-nine years old—until his baby-
making factory was shut down, his battery was broke, and
he could no longer do what men do and produce what men
produce. It was then that God gave Abraham a seed.

We won't understand God's plan unless we see that only
God could give Abraham the seed that hit Sarah's ninety-

year-old barren womb. Remember that by this time they were just two wrinkled old folks sitting around the house with an unused stack of diapers. In the words of the Bible, they "were old and well stricken in age; and it ceased to be with Sarah after the manner of women" (Genesis 18:11). God came along and quickened that which was dead and brought it back to life again. Do you know that God has the power to take something that you reckoned to be dead and bring it back to life again?

Indulge me as I tell a bit more of their story. Abraham said to Sarah, "Hey, baby! I feel all right now! I don't need any Cialis or Viagra. I have a word from God, so come here!" Sarah could hardly believe that. I love how the Bible says this: "Therefore Sarah laughed within herself, saying, After I am waxed old shall I have *pleasure*, my lord being old also?" (Genesis 18:12, emphasis mine). That seed was so potent that when it hit Sarah's womb, it quickened it and brought it back to life, brought it back to life so strong and so powerful that the old woman's body came back together, her muscles began to tingle, and she experienced sexual pleasure again. Isaac was conceived, Sarah's breasts began to fill with milk, and in her advanced age, God gave her the strength to bring the miracle child into this world.

Isaac came forth from her womb and made the old woman laugh with amazement (see Genesis 21:6). This is the seed of Abraham that passes down through forty-two generations, finds a virgin named Mary, steps into her dressing room, wraps Himself in flesh and comes out and stands among us and says,

I am the seed of Abraham,
I am the root of Jesse,
I am the Lamb of God,
I am the Lion of the tribe of Judah,
I am the resurrection and the life,
and he that believeth in Me, though he were dead, yet
    shall he live.

When Jesus came, they struggled with knowing what to call Him. "For unto us a child is born, unto us a son is given: and the government shall be upon his shoulder: and his name shall be called Wonderful, Counsellor, The mighty God, The everlasting Father, The Prince of Peace" (Isaiah 9:6). The angel Gabriel told Mary that the child was a "holy thing" (Luke 1:34). He was saying, "I don't know exactly what to call the child. Often God does something for which we have no name. He's just a holy thing."

Yes, Jesus is the seed of Abraham, the son of David,

Ruth's ultimate Kinsman Redeemer, the day star referred to by Peter, the wheel in the middle of the wheel in the book of Ezekiel. Jesus is my doctor, my lawyer, my turtledove, my fish and loaves, my Feast of Unleavened Bread, my sword and shield and buckler, and my scapegoat. He is the one who has stood in my place as a sinner and took the whipping for me.

But for the purpose of God's restoring us to Himself, there was a name that drew my attention. "And they shall call his name Emmanuel, which being interpreted is, God with us" (Matthew 1:23). "Emmanu" means "with us." "El" refers to Elohim, or God. *Emmanu-el* is "God tabernacled *with* us"—not above us or somewhere nearby. All of us are included. God is meeting us in a specific

> *Emmanuel is God's rendezvous with humanity. He is the place we're going to meet.*

place. Emmanuel is God's rendezvous with humanity. He is the place we're going to meet.

In the words of today, we might say, "Are you available tonight, baby? I want to take you out. Put on that red dress, the one you wear with the red stilettos. Pull your hair back the way I like it, and meet me." Emmanuel is the place where we meet God. It literally means "the tent of meeting," where God meets man to get back what was lost. It references the Old Testament tabernacle in the wilderness, which was a shadow or symbol of which Christ is the reality.

The Tabernacle and Jesus

God's dating with mankind began with Abraham and carried on through the seed of Abraham, the nation of Israel. From the land of Egypt and the captivity of Pharaoh, God took Israel into the wilderness so He could date them. All the wilderness experience was about God dating Israel. At the start of this date, He showed them how strong He was. When Israel became hungry, God became bread of heaven; when Israel asked for meat, He called for the quail to literally fly into their camp (Exodus 16); when Israel became thirsty, He became water out of a rock (Exodus 17). When we're on a date with God, sometimes He does stuff for us to show how "bad" He is, how we don't need any other lover to provide for us. That was certainly the case with the Israelites.

Out in the middle of the desert, the hot sand felt like needles in the Israelites' feet, and the temperatures were so severe that they could not last more than a day walking over the parched ground. There was no water for miles, there was nothing green, and people passed out, envisioning water they could not find and a life they could not reach. God dated Israel in the most despicable conditions imaginable, because His strength is made perfect in their weakness. If God ever takes us on a date, we should expect to get into trouble, because God looks the best when life looks the worst. When our lives are crumbling into pieces, we can see more clearly who God is.

> *If God ever takes us on a date, we should expect to get into trouble.*

When our friends leave us and our families forsake us, we know who God is. God will pick us up.

There in the parched desert, after God had given Moses the commandments on Mount Sinai, He instructed Moses, "Build a tent in the middle of the desert, because I am going to date Israel in the wilderness." God gave exacting details for both the building of the tabernacle as well as the items within the tabernacle, and He promised the tabernacle was "where I will meet you, to speak there unto thee" (Exodus 29:42). All of the tribes of Israel pitched their tents around the tabernacle, for there in the middle of the desert God decided to throw a party, a place of redemption, as a shadow of what Christ would one day accomplish.

There in the tabernacle, in the cold blight of night and the scorching heat of day, God arranged a special date with Israel. There the Shekinah (the place where God dwells), glory of God descended on the Holy of Holies and all the tribes of Israel gathered around it. "Then a cloud covered the tent of the congregation, and the glory of the LORD filled the tabernacle. And Moses was not able to enter into the tent of the congregation, because the cloud abode thereon, and the glory of the LORD filled the tabernacle" (Exodus 40:34–35). They could see God's glory, but they could not touch it. They couldn't get close to God, because there was still a gulf between them.

Like a bird and a fish, God and the Israelites could not connect. But God said, "I will get as close to you as the blood of bullocks and goats will allow, so You can see My glory from a distance." So the Israelites sat in the doorways of their tents and looked at a God whom they couldn't touch. Intimacy was denied by the flagrancy of sin. In the metaphor of the bird and the fish, a bird looked down and saw a fish, but the bird couldn't swim. The fish looked up saw a bird, but the fish couldn't fly. So they tried to be happy just being "close." God was finding a way to get close to man, because man could not find a way to get close to God. Christ is the only way to get to God.

What the tabernacle was in the Old Testament, Christ is in reality. I could go into great detail about how the Levite priests entered the tabernacle to represent the children of Israel. They would go past the outer court and the brazen altar and the brazen laver and into the Most Holy Place, where the table of showbread and the golden candlestick stood, as well as the altar of incense, which represented the prayers of the saints. Only on the great day of Atonement was the high priest allowed to pass through the veil and enter the Holy of Holies, which was where the fire of God fell and the Ark of the Covenant with the mercy seat was. Behind the thick veil, the high priest had access to God—only once a year—in order to ask for the forgiveness of the sins of the people. Everyone else had to stand outside. Even the priests dare not come in glibly, as did Aaron's sons, Nadab and Abihu in Leviticus 10 lest he die, for the veil in the temple blocked the way to God.

"Emmanuel, God with Us"

I hope you see that what the tabernacle was in abstraction, Christ is in reality. Instead of using a tent made out of goat-skins, Christ's body was the tent made of human flesh, and the Shekinah glory dwelt in His body rather sitting out on the rooftop. The apostle John could not have made it clearer: "And the Word was made flesh, and dwelt among us, (and we beheld his glory, the glory as of the only begotten of the Father,) full of grace and truth" (John 1:14). "God tabernacled with us," our Emmanuel.

The devil knew what Christ came to do and wanted to get Him out of the way before mankind could be restored to a relationship with God. But what he didn't know was that his hatred of Christ would play into God's plan. Believe it or not, sometimes it is God's will for people to hate us; in fact, He will use the script of their hate to manipulate His purpose, to move us to the right situation so He can work out His will in our lives. So let's not complain if some people don't like us, because sometimes God will make our enemies our footstool (see Psalm 110:1).

The apostle Paul said regarding Jesus' crucifixion, "But we speak the wisdom of God in a mystery, even the hidden wisdom, which God ordained before the world unto our glory: Which none of the princes of this world knew: for had they known it, they would not have crucified the Lord of glory" (1 Corinthians 2:7–8). They did not realize they were opening up a way for you and me to get to God!

Oh, thousands followed Jesus happily as long as He was healing folks, turning water into wine, and helping throw parties for people (John 2). He was cool.

He stopped the widow's funeral processional, touched

the bier, told the dead son to "Arise," and it was amazingly cool (Luke 7).

He stopped by when Lazarus was dead, wept when He saw the sisters' grief, then He cried with a loud voice, "Lazarus, come forth!" and it was all good (John 11).

The woman with the issue of blood touched the hem of His garment, and she was made perfectly well, and it was all good (Matthew 9).

While He was traveling from one city to the next, blind Bartimaeus stood by the side of the highway begging and cried out, "Jesus, Thou son of David, have mercy on me," and Jesus healed him, and it was all good (Mark 10).

One man stricken with an infirmity for thirty-seven years looked up at Jesus and said, "Sir, I have no man, when the water is troubled, to put me into the pool." Jesus told him, "Rise, take up thy bed, and walk," and it was all good (John 5).

It was all good until He approached the Cross.

Calvary's Cross

When Jesus got close to the Cross, the five thousand folks whom He had fed with loaves and fishes left Him, the cheering crowds moved away, those who followed closest started stepping back, and Bartimaeus was nowhere to be seen.

Jesus went to the Cross, but not before they beat Him severely. The prophet Isaiah said about Jesus, "There is no beauty that we should desire him" (Isaiah 53:2)—"no beauty" translates that they beat Him until shreds of His flesh opened up and His intestines bulged through His stomach. There was no beauty about Him. He was not the handsome Jesus we see artistically depicted on the Cross, with the covering of loincloth and the nicely orchestrated drips of blood falling from His side. Blood was gushing out of His body.

It was a miracle that Jesus even made it to the Cross and did not die on the whipping post when they scourged Him (John 19:1). History says that they beat Him with a cat-o'-nine-tails, so that when they lashed Him, it lacerated His flesh. A weaker person would have died on the whipping post. But if He had died there, He could not redeem man from the curse of the law and from sin and death, for He must be hung on a tree (see Galatians 3:13).

Then with the beard plucked from Jesus' face and a crown of thorns on his head, they thrust upon Him the Cross and He began the plight of carrying the Cross up the hill when He was too damaged to walk at all. He carried the Cross, stumbling in His gait as He walked. One man, a man of color, "a man of Cyrene" (Matthew 27:37), lifted the weight of the

Cross off Him, but the man did not know that it wasn't the weight of the wood that bore Him down; it was the weight of the sins of the world that bore Him down.

We stand at Calvary's Cross on Golgotha's hill—the darkest, most dismal, most bleak moment in all of the Holy Writ. The Romans were masters at torture. They laid down the Cross, put His hands on it, and drove nails into His hands—not into the fleshy part, but in the wrist area so that the nervous system would be irrupted and pain would shoot all through His body. These were not the nails you have in your house, but spikes that would hold together beams if you were building a railroad track. Then they crossed his feet and put a single nail through them. Part of the pain Jesus experienced on the Cross resulted from his pushing down on the nail in his feet in order to gasp a bit of air; then when the pain on his feet was too much, He sunk down, and the pain in His wrists shot horrifically through His body. He was fastened to the Cross with these. But don't think that it was the nails that held Him; it was His love for us that held Him to the Cross.

They hung Him high, and they stretched Him wide, and the ground got nervous and started trembling, and the sun turned its back and said, "I cannot watch this." All of hell stood at attention; demons were trembling. Ten thousand angels stood like archers waiting to be dispatched, but He didn't say a single word. The Roman soldiers gambled at the foot of the Cross for His garments; and when He said, "I thirst," they gave Him gall (vinegar mixed with water) to drink.

> *The ground got nervous and started trembling, and the sun turned its back and said, "I cannot watch this." All of hell stood at attention.*

The conflict of Christ's life had come to a perilous end, and now at the Cross we have the final trappings of truth that God has sent to us to accentuate the fact that Jesus died that we might have the right to access the tree of life again. And in His final agonizing moments, the chronicler Mark detailed for us the various aspects and predicaments of Christ, the Savior of the world, in the death process (see Mark 15:36–41):

> *And one ran and filled a spunge full of vinegar, and put it on a reed, and gave him to drink, saying, Let alone; let us see whether Elias will come to take him down.*
>
> *And Jesus cried with a loud voice, and gave up the ghost.*
>
> *And the veil of the temple was rent in twain from the top to the bottom.*

And when the centurion, which stood over against him, saw that he so cried out, and gave up the ghost, he said, Truly this man was the Son of God.

There were also women looking on afar off: among whom was Mary Magdalene, and Mary the mother of James the less and of Joses, and Salome; (who also, when he was in Galilee, followed him, and ministered unto him;) and many other women which came up with him unto Jerusalem.

The women came as close to Him as religion would allow, which was "afar off." Religion has always kept women from getting close to power. It was not just the "good" women, for there was Mary Magdalene, from whom Jesus had cast seven demons (see Luke 8:2). She came because He loved her when she was unlovely, and she stood in the crowd with the righteous women and loved Him from a distance. That the women are acknowledged here is significant because in Judaistic ideology, women were not recognized at all—it speaks to the emancipation of the feminine spirit. Mark was careful to acknowledge women at the Cross, for Christ fuses together the male and the female, the Gentile and the Jew, the bond and the free, in a unique and powerful way.

The Roman soldiers cared nothing for the dying men on the crosses and tired of waiting to leave, so they broke the legs of the men hanging on the crosses nearby Jesus who were not dead. They broke their legs because the crucified ones would use their legs to push their weight up so that they could keep breathing. When their legs were broken, the men quickly died from asphyxiation as the full weight of their body collapsed their lungs.

But when they came to Jesus, He was already obedient unto death. He had already said yes to death, so no bones were broken in His body; for if they had broken one bone in His body, He would have been rejected as the Sacrificial Lamb, for the law says no bones can be broken in His body. To make certain Christ was dead, one soldier took his spear, thrust it into Christ's side, and the Bible says out of His side came blood and water (see John 19:34). He had been dead so long that congealing had taken place, the separation of the red corpuscles from the white.

This brings me to the point I want you to see regarding what happened on the hill called Calvary. When Jesus "cried with a loud voice, and gave up the ghost," the veil that hung between the Holy of Holies and the Most Holy Place in the temple "was rent in twain from the top to the bottom" (Matthew 27:51). Like the tabernacle, the temple was also a shadow or symbol of which Christ was the reality. There was a communication between that which was former and that which is new. When Jesus took His last breath upon the Cross, the veil was rent where no human hand could reach, because what the veil was in the shadow, Christ was in reality.

The veil in the temple was rent, not so that God could get out but that we could get in! The door was opened.

Access Is Granted!

Thus, the Cross is the hinge of salvation and fellowship with God. The Cross makes the door open so we can have access to God. If there is no Cross, there is no hinge. If there is no hinge, there is no door. Without a door, there is no access.

The Cross is the place where mercy and truth meet together.

The Cross is the place where law and grace stand up against each other. What causes law and grace to connect is the Cross.

The Cross is the place where sinners come to the Savior.

The Cross is the place where the lost find their way.

The Cross is the place where the spiritually blind receive their sight.

The Cross is the place where the corrupt and depraved become saints.

That is the power of the Cross! The veil was ripped open!

We don't have to stand back as Israel did and watch
the Shekinah glory from afar off.
We don't need to go to the priest to find absolution for
our sins, because God has opened up the door of
forgiveness.
We do not need to come from a religious background
to qualify.

We can come to God, smelling like a bag of dope. Religion would say, "Come no closer," but the veil in the temple
was ripped so completely that it could not be stitched back together again. So the most degraded person in the world can come to God and say, "Just as I am without one plea, but that thy blood was shed for me, and that thou bidst me come to thee, O Lamb of God, I come, I come."

> *Even the most degraded person in the world can come to God and say, "Just as I am without one plea, but that thy blood was shed for me."*

If you don't praise Jesus Christ right now, you are a fool, because He ripped it for you and for me! God ripped the veil for us. The access gained is so wide open that the book of Hebrews states, "Let us therefore come boldly unto the throne of grace, that we may obtain mercy, and find grace to help in time of need" (Hebrews 4:16).

When Adam and Eve left Him and the Garden of Eden, they were bowed with shame. But now we can come boldly before Him to the throne of grace!

Do Not Hold Back

How is it possible that we hold back from coming to Jesus? As we've said before, for the bird and fish who have fallen in love, God has created a place for them to meet—God and man, divinity and humanity, celestial and terrestrial. Christ was man enough to be nursed at the breast of Mary, yet He was God enough to create the milk He drank. He was man enough to die on the Cross, but God enough to create the tree that became the Cross. He was man enough to stumble under the weight of going up the hill to Calvary, but He was God enough to create the hill. Jesus Christ is not the good man; He is the God man. Jesus is the place of connection. He is the place where the divine and the human come together. He is the place where our healing begins.

Don't get tricked into coming to church for entertainment or to get your dance on or to get your praise on, because that club mentality has to go. If you want to party and dance and be entertained, find it elsewhere. The true Gospel is about us being restored to a relationship with the God who made us for His glory.

Perhaps you sense that something is missing out of your life, and nothing you have tried has filled in the vacuum. You've done this and that and the other, and it has not worked. You may have even tried church, but there is a difference between trying church and trying Jesus. Hear me, and hear me good, the same enemy who sidetracked Adam and Eve knows when you're responding to Christ. He will distract you any way he can from coming in faith. He'll make you nervous about what others will think, and he'll make you worry about what needs to change in your life, because he knows he is about to lose his grip on your life. Satan will try to stop you, to hold you, to paralyze you, to give you fear, to tell you you're not ready. But the devil is a liar!

Jesus Christ offers you what you will never find in any drug or drink or relationship or thing, and He offers it to you for free. Your soul knows that something is missing. You may have tried to find it in the arms of lovers, but no one can give you what you are missing. You got mad at them and walked away and tried another and another. But the real Lover is waiting. He is the Lover of your soul, and your soul misses Him. Nothing you build, buy, drive, shoot, snort, hook, deal, or play will ever replace the void in your heart, as long as you are separated from the Master.

I'm not calling you to me, because I'm not better than you. I'm not calling you to a church, because the church is no Savior. I'm not calling you to a denomination, because I'm sick of all of them. I'm not calling you to religion, because I'm tired of religion, too. But I am calling you into a relationship with the Savior. He is waiting to get you back. He is waiting to renew what you lost. He is waiting to give back what got away from you. He's waiting on you.

If your spouse won't come to Jesus, come alone. If you can't get the kids to want Jesus, go for it yourself. If your mamma won't come, come by yourself. For now is the moment of salvation, now is the moment when redemption is offered, now is the moment when the transformation occurs. If your soul is thirsty, broken, bruised, and bleeding, come to Jesus. Bring your problems to Jesus, and bring your crisis to Jesus.

No matter what you've done or how bad you feel, Jesus has ripped the veil and opened the door of access to God. All that the first Adam gave away, the second Adam has restored. Come boldly in the name of Jesus, confess your sins, and have your unrighteousness washed away in the blood of Jesus.

Thousands of years went into restoring access
so that sneaky creeps such as you and me
can come boldly into God's loving presence
as children of God.

Jesus gave His life on the Cross
to make it happen.

Do you know what shocks God,
what breaks His heart today?

It's when you and I stand there looking
and won't come in.

CHRIST, WHO, BEING THE HOLIEST
AMONG THE MIGHTY, AND
MIGHTIEST AMONG THE HOLY,
LIFTED WITH HIS PIERCED HANDS
EMPIRES OFF THEIR HINGES
AND TURNED THE STREAM OF
CENTURIES OUT OF ITS CHANNEL,
AND STILL GOVERNS THE AGES.

—*Jean Paul (J. P. F. Richter)*

THE CROSS—A SYMBOL OF EVIL

While I was preaching the messages that formed the foundation for this book, my fourteen-year-old son and I were talking, and he was saying he was excited about the Cross. I was thrilled with that, of course, and I said to him what I also say to you, "Son, I'm only scraping the surface. If I talked the rest of my life until the day that I die, I still would not be able to tell you all that Jesus did on the Cross when He died for us. It is more than a story. Most of us know the biblical account that surrounds Easter, but I want you to understand the reality: Here hinges the framework of all that we will ever do or be; we are recipients thereof, through the grace of the Cross."

I was reminded of the revelation that the prophet Isaiah was given concerning the Cross and the Man of Sorrows more than seven hundred years before it came to pass. He wrote these heartrending words: "Who hath believed our report? and to whom is the arm of the LORD revealed? For he shall grow up before him as a tender plant, and as a root out of a dry ground: he hath no form nor comeliness; and when we shall see him, there is no beauty that we should desire him. He is despised and rejected of men; a man of sorrows, and acquainted with grief: and we hid as it were our faces from him; he was despised, and we esteemed him not. Surely he hath borne our griefs, and carried our sorrows: yet we did esteem him stricken, smitten of God, and afflicted" (Isaiah 53:1–4).

It's almost as if Isaiah is asking the question, How does a Savior who is so good, so worthy of praise, bear our griefs and carry our sorrows and end up smitten of God and afflicted? In the light of such a profound truth, I asked the Father, in the name of Jesus, to give me grace to minister this Word to you powerfully, effectively, and succinctly. I asked God for the nimbleness of thought that I might definitively declare His Word and make it so simple that a child can understand and yet so revelatory and so profound that professors cannot escape the grasp of God's auspicious grace. Amen.

The Power of Symbolism

Wherever we go today, there are symbols everywhere that carry subliminal messages. A symbol is a visible sign or representation of an idea or quality or of another object. They make us aware of certain things without the need for speech or evidence. When we're driving down the road and see a bright bold red target symbol, no one needs to shout out that we're passing a Target store. Symbolism is a powerful tool, whether we are talking about the Golden Arches or the Eiffel Tower. The moment we see the Eiffel Tower, we know we're not in Dallas; and the moment we see the Golden Arches, we know we're not at Wendy's.

Symbolism conveys a message, identifies a person, place, or thing, and brings us into an awareness of a reality that subliminally tells us that when we see this, expect that. Symbolism is very important. Millions and millions of dollars are spent every year to bring together the brightest minds and designers

> *Symbolism subliminally tells us that when we see this, expect that.*

to develop logos, brands, and concepts that are synonymous with the ideals of the companies or the industries that are being projected to their audiences. Utmost attention is given to make sure that there is no disconnect between the creator of the logo and the beholder, so the beholder instantly perceives the message through the symbol. Thus, when I say "the Big Apple," you know I'm not talking about Chicago; when I say "the Windy City," you know I'm not talking about New York.

Symbolism is very, very important, and not just in business, not just in the secular realm, but also very important in the Scriptures. God uses symbols to help us understand things about Him that we would not otherwise understand. For instance, in the Old Testament, the Ark of the Covenant was an outstanding symbol. When the children of Israel came near the Ark of the Covenant, it represented the very presence of God. The Israelites carried the Ark of the Covenant with them into battle with a shout so loud it shook the ground (see 1 Samuel 4:5), and when they marched around the city of Jericho before its walls fell down, they carried the Ark in procession (see Joshua 6). They did so because they felt that if they had the symbol, the Lord of Hosts was with them.

The Bible is filled with symbols. Both oil and wind are powerful images that often represent the presence of God. Water is used to represent the Word of God. The number seven is used to represent perfection or excellence, and the number four represents completion (thus the four winds, the seven churches, the seven seals). The color white often represents purity, the color red can represent bloodshed, purple may represent royalty, and gold designates deity. These are all very powerful symbols and metaphors.

However, keep in mind that the symbol is not what it represents. If it was, you could eat the Golden Arches. If it was, you could take a plane to a big apple. There is a difference between the symbol and what it represents.

What the Cross Represents

When we come to the Cross, among the many things that it represents, it does not represent the presence of God— if anything, it represents the absence of God's presence. How can I say that? Because Christ Himself cried out with a loud voice from the Cross, *"Eli, Eli, lama sabachthani?"* which is, being interpreted, "My God, my God, why hast thou forsaken me?" (Matthew 27:46).

So if the Cross is not given to us to represent the presence of God, what does it represent? For one thing, the Cross is a powerful symbol of God's judgment of sin. You may argue it represents salvation, but I would argue back that you cannot have salvation without judgment; for it is the fact that it represents judgment that makes me eligible to be a recipient of salvation. You may say it represents love, but I say it represents anger, because if God was expressing love, why was Christ "smitten of God?" In both instances, I would argue that we are both right. But we are looking at it from two different sides. You are looking at it from the earthly side; I am describing it from the heavenly side. I am looking at it from God's perspective.

Isaiah taught us that Christ on the Cross was smitten of God. What is it about this symbol that we are missing? We understand that the blood of Jesus was shed; we understand that we were redeemed; we understand that "God so loved the world, that he gave his only begotten Son" (John 3:16); we understand that the blood is the price of redemption; we understand that through it Jesus becomes the Kinsman Redeemer; we understand that the Cross is the hinge that connects Judaism with Christianity, and we understand that without the Cross there is no door whereby salvation is offered. Nevertheless, we are missing something vital that we need to know.

The Seed of the Woman and the Seed of the Serpent

I want to go back to Genesis 3 and review the first fifteen verses that we've already studied, but consider them in a different light. As you read through the biblical account, I have boldfaced every time you see "the serpent." If you read carefully, you'll see that it is used five times in this short section.

> Now **the serpent** was more subtil than any beast of the field which the LORD God had made. And he said unto the woman, Yea, hath God said, Ye shall not eat of every tree of the garden?
>
> And the woman said unto **the serpent**, We may eat of the fruit of the trees of the garden: But of the fruit of the tree which is in the midst of the garden, God hath said, Ye shall not eat of it, neither shall ye touch it, lest ye die.
>
> And **the serpent** said unto the woman, Ye shall not surely die: For God doth know that in the day ye eat thereof, then your eyes shall be opened, and ye shall be as gods, knowing good and evil.
>
> And when the woman saw that the tree was good for food, and that it was pleasant to the eyes, and a tree to be desired to make one wise, she took of the fruit thereof, and did eat, and gave also unto her husband with her; and he did eat. And the eyes of them both were opened, and they knew that they were naked; and they sewed fig leaves together, and made themselves aprons.
>
> And they heard the voice of the LORD God walking in the garden in the cool of the day: and Adam and his wife hid themselves from the presence of the LORD God amongst the trees of the garden.
>
> And the LORD God called unto Adam, and said unto him, Where art thou?

And he said, I heard thy voice in the garden, and I was afraid, because I was naked; and I hid myself.

And he said, Who told thee that thou wast naked? Hast thou eaten of the tree, whereof I commanded thee that thou shouldest not eat?

And the man said, The woman whom thou gavest to be with me, she gave me of the tree, and I did eat.

And the LORD *God said unto the woman, What is this that thou hast done?*

And the woman said, **The serpent** *beguiled me, and I did eat.*

And the LORD *God said unto* **the serpent***, Because thou hast done this, thou art cursed above all cattle, and above every beast of the field; upon thy belly shalt thou go, and dust shalt thou eat all the days of thy life:*

And I will put enmity between thee and the woman, and between thy seed and her seed; it shall bruise thy head, and thou shalt bruise his heel.

Although we explored these verses in the previous chapters, I now draw your special attention to the last verse. Notice that at this point, neither the woman nor the serpent have a "seed." Here we need to understand the symbols that God is using. He starts out talking to the serpent—the symbol, the icon—but He ends up addressing what the icon represents. To the icon, which is the serpent that Satan used, He said, "Upon thy belly shalt thou go, and dust shalt thou eat all the days of thy life." He compares the serpent to cattle. There He is dealing with the physical serpent. But when He says, "I will put enmity between thee and the woman, and between thy seed and her seed," He is dealing with what the symbol represents, which is Satan operating through the serpent.

Warfare Between the Seed of the Serpent and the Seed of the Woman

In Genesis 3:15, we are dealing with the first prophetic messianic promise concerning Jesus Christ, because Christ is the seed of the woman. The woman doesn't have a seed—Christ is the seed. Clearly, God is stating, "I am going to put warfare between the seed of the serpent and the seed of the woman," and the rest of the Bible is the story of that battle.

What we are reading about is two conversations. God curses the symbol and says, "Dust shalt thou eat all the days of thy life"—that's a life span for the physical serpent, then it's gone. But what He deals with next is what the symbol represents, and He becomes prophetic, because we are going to be dealing with Satan throughout ages and ages, not through a life span.

It is crucial to understand how God deals with what that symbol represents. When He deals with the devil behind the symbol, He says, "I will put enmity between thee and the woman, and between thy seed and her seed."

If we were to expand the reach of this book, I would go into a comprehensive study of "the seed of Satan," because you must understand that Satan operates in a trinity similar to God, *First,* he is the fallen "Lucifer, son of the morning" (Isaiah 14:12), so he is satanic in his main operation. *Second,* he also operates as the antichrist when he embodies himself in physical form, similar to how God manifests Himself through Jesus Christ. Satan comes through the antichrist as "the man of sin be revealed, the son of perdition; Who opposeth and exalteth himself above all that is called God, or that is worshipped; so that he as God sitteth in the temple of God, shewing himself that he is God" (2 Thessalonians 2:3–4). Then, *third,* similar to how God works and moves through the Holy Spirit, in the End Times, Satan begins to operate through "the false prophet that wrought miracles before him" in the book of Revelation (19:20).

Notice that when God begins to curse Satan, He curses him from his origin to his destiny and all the manifestations in between. There will be war between the seed of the woman and the seed of the serpent, and that is why over and over throughout history, we see Satan operating through different people trying to kill the woman's child as described in Revelation 12:1–5:

> *There appeared a great wonder in heaven; a woman clothed with the sun, and the moon under her feet, and upon her head a crown of twelve stars: And she being with child cried, travailing in birth, and pained to be delivered. And there appeared another wonder in heaven; and behold a great red dragon, having seven heads and ten horns, and seven crowns upon his heads. And his tail drew the third part of the stars of heaven, and did cast them to the earth: and the dragon stood before the woman which was ready to be delivered, for to devour her child as soon as it was born. And she brought forth a man child, who was to rule all nations with a rod of iron: and her child was caught up unto God, and to his throne.*

Satan Tried to Kill the Seed

We see the prolific use of symbols in these verses from Revelation. Satan, the serpent, the great red dragon, is always out to destroy "the child of the woman." That is why when Moses was about to be born, there was a decree made that all the male children were to be killed up to the age of two years old. Satan was trying to kill the

> *Satan will always try to kill the seed of your promise before it reaches fruition.*

seed before it reached fruition (see Exodus 1:22). That is the way he operates—he will always try to kill the seed of your promise before it reaches fruition. The battle never ceases.

Even when Christ was coming, Satan was aware that He was coming, and he sent out a death decree through Herod the Great: "When he saw that he was mocked of the wise men, was exceeding wroth, and sent forth, and slew all the children that were in Bethlehem, and in all the coasts thereof, from two years old and under, according to the time which he had diligently inquired of the wise men" (Matthew 2:16). Why was Satan killing all those children? Satan doesn't mind whom or how many, he kills as long as he can kill the seed. All this killing and destruction is birthed through "the serpent." The serpent is the symbol of evil: the slithering, crawling, hissing sound is the symbol of the treacherous, demonic influence of Satan. "The serpent . . . the serpent . . . the serpent . . ."

A Stick and a Serpent

We see the serpent again when Moses is in the wilderness having an encounter with God. God said to Moses, "What is that in thine hand? And he said, A rod. And he said, Cast it on the ground. And he cast it on the ground, and it became a serpent; and Moses fled from before it" (Exodus 4:2–3). Did you notice that when Moses' rod turned into a serpent, Moses ran? Even in Moses' generation, thousands of years after The Fall in the Garden, the serpent was still a symbol of evil. It's not that Moses was afraid of snakes, but he knew that the snake represented evil; and because it represented evil, he did not want to touch it. God had to call him back and instruct him to pick it up by the tail, and it turned back into a stick.

A *stick* and a *serpent*. Put a pin in your mind there, because we are going to see that over and over again. There will always be the slithering of the snake and the rigidity of the stick. There is some collaboration, some connection between a stick and a serpent. Moses threw a stick down, and it became a serpent. He picked it up again, and it became a stick. Think about the third chapter of Genesis: This describes the entire conflict between the seed of the woman who would one day die on the stick and the seed of the serpent that would embody evil. All throughout Scripture, you will see the symbolism of the stick and the snake.

The serpent is the symbol of

> *The serpent is the symbol of evil, and wherever he goes he tries to destroy and tries to lead to the demise of the seed of woman.*

evil, and wherever he goes he tries to destroy and tries to lead to the demise of the seed of woman, because the serpent is the symbol of all that Satan wants to do in the earth.

"As Moses Lifted Up the Serpent"

Interestingly, when Jesus begins His ministry, He draws a parallel between Himself and the serpent. Let me introduce this thought with an old hymn title from my Baptist roots, "Lift Him Up," that was written by Johnson Oatman Jr.

How to reach the masses, men of every birth,
For an answer, Jesus gave the key:
"And I, if I be lifted up from the earth,
Will draw all men unto Me."

Lift Him up, lift Him up,
Still He speaks from eternity:
"And I, if I be lifted up from the earth,
Will draw all men unto Me."

Oh! the world is hungry for the Living Bread,
Lift the Savior up for them to see;

Trust Him, and do not doubt the words that He said,

"I'll draw all men unto Me."

Lift Him up, lift Him up,

Still He speaks from eternity:

"And I, if I be lifted up from the earth,

Will draw all men unto Me."

I've sung that hymn for years, but what does it mean? Jesus said, "And as Moses lifted up the serpent in the wilderness, even so must the Son of man be lifted up: That whosoever believeth in him should not perish, but have eternal life" (John 3:14–15). Something that happened with Moses in the wilderness became a symbol of what would happen with Christ, and it is crucial that we understand it.

How did Moses lift up the serpent in the wilderness? Let's get the background for the story of the Israelites as told in Numbers 21:4–9.

And they journeyed from mount Hor by the way of the Red sea, to compass the land of Edom: and the soul of the people was much discouraged because of the way. And the people spake against God, and against Moses, Where-

fore have ye brought us up out of Egypt to die in the wilderness? for there is no bread, neither is there any water; and our soul loatheth this light bread.

And the LORD sent fiery serpents among the people, and they bit the people; and much people of Israel died.

Therefore the people came to Moses, and said, We have sinned, for we have spoken against the LORD, and against thee; pray unto the LORD, that he take away the serpents from us. And Moses prayed for the people.

And the LORD said unto Moses, Make thee a fiery serpent, and set it upon a pole: and it shall come to pass, that every one that is bitten, when he looketh upon it, shall live.

And Moses made a serpent of brass, and put it upon a pole, and it came to pass, that if a serpent had bitten any man, when he beheld the serpent of brass, he lived.

This Old Testament account is an amazing symbol of what Christ accomplished on the Cross. In order for the brass to look like the serpents that bit the people, the brass had to be beaten. If it had not been beaten, the brass would not have changed its form and turned into the thing that bit the people. The beating of the brass is a picture of the judgment of God that took Christ and formed Him into the thing that bit the people. Follow me closely as I explain what I mean!

After Moses had beaten the brass and turned it into the serpent, he *lifted the serpent up.* I said this previously: Isn't it amazing that Christ did not die on the whipping post at the hands of the Romans? History says that He was beaten so severely that He should have died before He reached the Cross. They beat Him with a cat-o'-nine-tails to the point that His intestines were hanging out. If He had

> *History says that He was beaten so severely that He should have died before He reached the Cross.*

died on the whipping post, He would not have been lifted up; and if He had not been lifted up, we would not have been delivered from sin. Christ resisted death and held death back. They pulled His beard out of His face, blood was running down His chin and face, but He refused to die, because He had to make this correlation between the stick and the serpent. And when they nailed Him to the tree and hung Him high, when they stretched Him wide and lifted Him up, He became on the Cross a picture of what the serpent was in the wilderness.

Where did I come up with this? Jesus said, "And as Moses lifted up the serpent in the wilderness, even so must the Son of man be lifted up."

Go back to the people of Israel who were dying in the wilderness. God says, "I'm going to cure you with what you are dying from. You've been bitten and poisoned with the venom of the snakes, and the antidote is going to be made from the same venom that's killing you." Even today, when a snake bites a person, the antidote is made from the very poison of the venom.

I was talking with a person who had the flu recently, and I asked if he had gotten a flu shot. He replied, "No, I'm afraid of the flu shot." Now, I'm not trying to persuade you regarding vaccinations, but just follow the metaphor. The flu vaccine is made from the flu. By injecting into you what you are trying to get away from, your resistance against getting infected by what you are trying to escape is built up. This is not a new idea. For when the people of Israel were bitten by the poisonous snakes, God said, "I'm going to cure you with what is killing you."

He didn't lift up a dove; that wouldn't have done it.
He didn't lift up the wind; that wouldn't have done it.
He didn't lift up water; that wouldn't have done it.

No, God said, "I'm going to lift up the very evil that you are infected by." Scripture says that if the brazen serpent was lifted up, and all those who were dying on the ground in the desert with parched throats, scorching fevers, and hallucinations, if they would look up—please read these words closely—they would find healing! Come on! I'm showing you what Jesus did on the Cross to bring about deliverance for you!

I want you to see that the serpent, the brazen serpent, becomes the savior to the people. The brass was made into a serpent; but when it was beaten and then lifted up, it became a savior to the people. And if anyone looked at it, they were saved from the poison that was killing them. Even today, modern medicine uses the symbol of a stick and snake to represent healing. So when you go to the doctor's office, on the medical certificates on the wall of his or her practice, the symbol that represents healing is a stick with a snake.

I hope you are saying, "Hallelujah!" You don't have to tell me what's poisoned you; you don't have to tell me what's wrong with you; you don't have to tell me that you're twisted by sin or depraved, because that is true of every one of us. Rather, just say, "I'm looking up to Jesus. God is healing me! He's healing me!" Yes! And if we can just look up when all hell is breaking loose and trouble is everywhere and the storms of life are raging! If we can just look up, we can be healed! So Moses made the serpent out of brass, he lifted it up, and the people were healed.

Remarkably, long years later, King Hezekiah would have to destroy the brazen serpent. "He removed the high places, and brake the images, and cut down the groves, and brake in pieces the brasen serpent that Moses had made: for unto those days the children of Israel did burn incense to it: and he called it Nehushtan" (2 Kings 18:4). By this time the people began to worship the symbol and missed the reality of which the symbol was only a schoolmaster. We do the same today, by the way. When we make a god out of whomever God has used to help you, for instance: God will snatch them away and say, "I will not share My glory with another."

Here's the point: Only God can take what is wrong with us and use it to heal us! He will take the very one who broke our hearts and use what that person did to heal our hearts! You have to live awhile to know what I'm talking about. God is in the business of making the antidote from the venom. When the serpent is lifted up, it transitions and becomes the savior. Even as a snake is biting you on the ankle, you are looking up at a snake; and the snake you are looking up at is healing you from the snake that is poisoning you, because when it becomes lifted up, it saves you from what you went through.

Jesus Was Made Sin for Us

If we don't understand this transition, we will never comprehend the Cross. The apostle Paul states, "For he hath made him to be sin for us, who knew no sin; that we might be made the righteousness of God in him" (2 Corinthians 5:21). Do you see what God is doing here? "He hath made him to be sin for us" means Christ became sin for us without ever sinning.

Jesus Christ never lied, but He became a lie for me.
He wasn't an adulterer, but He became adultery for me.

He didn't commit the act, but He symbolized the act when He was lifted up on the Cross. On the Cross, Jesus becomes the epitome of every wicked, nasty, evil, treacherous, dirty thing anyone has ever done—not just what we have done, but anything we will ever do, and anything that prison inmates have done, and anything any abuser or rapist or killer or murderer have done.

Jesus Christ "became sin"—He had to cover every sin and all unrighteousness, or the Cross would mean nothing. He couldn't become adultery and not become homosexuality. He couldn't become homosexuality and not become a lie, because if He did, we could only preach the Gospel to the specific groups of people who qualify.

Do you see it? Christ became sin! He became sin for you and me! Watch this right here. We are looking up, and we see a wondrous Savior; but God is looking down, and He sees sin! We are looking up, and we see pure righteousness; God is looking at the Cross, and He sees wickedness!

The Cross was so horrific to Christ that He prayed three times: "O my Father, if this cup may not pass away from me, except I drink it, thy will be done" (Matthew 26:42). Do you think He was afraid of death? No, He woke Lazarus up from the dead on the way to the Cross (see John 11:43). He wasn't afraid of death! Do you think He was afraid of the nails? No! He made the steel that formed the nails! You don't see Him praying, "Oh, Father, these nails are too much! O Father, this Cross is too much!"

No, but He does ask God why He forsook Him. From heaven's point of view, God had to forsake Him because in that moment Jesus became the symbol for every wicked, lustful, craving, devious, conniving, satanic, witchcraft-endorsing, child-molesting, raping, murdering, serial-killing, mass-suicide, national-genocide activity that could ever happen in the world. He became the icon that God had to smite to be able to save us, and suddenly the Lamb of God was smitten! "He was smitten of God," so that all our sins and all

> *From heaven's point of view, Jesus became the symbol for every wicked, lustful, conniving, satanic, witchcraft-endorsing, child-molesting, raping, murdering activity that could ever happen in the world.*

our iniquities could be laid on Him. When the Father reared back and slapped Jesus, He was really slapping our sins.

The Good News!

So now comes the good news: "There is therefore now no condemnation to them which are in Christ Jesus, who walk not after the flesh, but after the Spirit" (Romans 8:1). In our judicial system, we cannot try a man twice for the same crime. Once we have executed judgment on him, we cannot come back and judge him again for the same thing, because the second judgment would not be just. So if Christ became the embodiment of my sins, and God judged it on

> *God cannot judge me when He already judged me two thousand years ago!*

Calvary, then I am free from my sins as long as I cast them on Calvary. God cannot judge me when He already judged me two thousand years ago!

As the serpent in the wilderness became a savior, so the Christ who was the Savior on the Cross became a serpent. He became sin who knew no sin, so everyone who had been bitten and poisoned by sin could look up at Him and be saved.

Again, from the old hymn by Johnson Oatman Jr:

How to reach the masses, men of every birth,

For an answer, Jesus gave the key:

"And I, if I be lifted up from the earth,

Will draw all men unto Me."

Remember I said if "the princes of this world" had known, "they would not have crucified the Lord of glory" (1 Corinthians 2:8). Because if they hadn't crucified Him, He wouldn't have been lifted up. If He had not been lifted up, Satan would have won!

Lift Him up, lift Him up,

Still He speaks from eternity:

"And I, if I be lifted up from the earth,

Will draw all men unto Me."

Because Christ became sin for all of us, I can preach the same Gospel in the White House as in a crack house. I can preach the same Gospel in the opulence of Geneva as I can in the bush country of Ghana. I went into the bush in Ghana and stepped over dead goats and chickens' blood to minister to a witch doctor. And I didn't need to find another Savior, because the same blood that was shed for my mess was shed for him.

Yes, I believe abortion is wrong. I believe it is sin. I believe it is taking of life! I believe it, and I know there are many women reading my words who have had abortions. I understand that, but that was on the Cross, too.

It is not God's will for us to divorce and remarry, and to do the things that we do the way that we do them, because we are breaking a covenant and an oath we made before God; but that was on the Cross, too!

As hideous and horrible as is the sin of the child molester, that was on the Cross, too!

We have teams of people from our church that go into prisons; and we minister to people on death row who have committed unthinkable murders, because that was on the Cross, too.

> *Whatever you think about,*
>
> *whatever you are being,*
>
> *whatever you are ashamed of,*
>
> *whatever you imagine,*
>
> *whatever you came from,*

whatever wakes you up in the middle of the night—
Christ did not leave that sin out;
it was included on the Cross!

Read the words of the prophet Isaiah once again: "Surely he hath borne our griefs, and carried our sorrows: yet we did esteem him stricken, smitten of God, and afflicted." I encourage you at this very moment to shout it out: *"Surely! Surely! Surely! Surely! Surely He hath borne our griefs, and carried our sorrows!"*

Isaiah must have said to himself, "I don't understand what I am seeing. I see it from such a distance. How can He be so good and yet be smitten of God? How is it possible, God?" It was because Isaiah was looking at the Cross from the bottom up. God was looking from heaven down.

He Was Smitten and Died

Lest we forget it, I must add that Christ died for us.

When they lifted Him up on the Cross, I believe the ground trembled because it had never seen so much sin concentrated in one place. When the sun went dark, I believe it was saying, "I can't look at Him. I have never seen so much evil in one place!" But this dynamic is neither the physical ground nor the sounds of embarrassment. There was something that happened in the spirit world when Jesus was smitten of God.

I need to take you deeper into the heart of what happened. The Cross is to us what the brazen altar was in the Jewish temple. The brazen altar was the place where sin was dealt with. A man would bring his lamb and take it to the brazen altar, where it would be tied to the altar. There would be a pan to catch the blood and fire to burn the flesh. The priest would raise the knife to slay the lamb, because the lamb was an offering for the man's sins. The lamb did not die because it was innocent; it died because it had taken on the sins of the man. I know that God did not kill the lamb's innocence, because the innocence that was on the lamb went onto the man, so that the sins that were on the man could go onto the lamb. If you want to know how alive the man was, check how dead the lamb was. The lamb was killed because the lamb was what the man used to be; and God let the man live because the man became the innocence that the lamb had before it died.

Thus Paul could say, "I am crucified with Christ: nevertheless I live; yet not I, but Christ liveth in me: and the life which I now live in the flesh I live by the faith of the Son of God, who loved me, and gave himself for me" (Galatians 2:20).

I cannot teach the consequences of the Cross and not

teach it in such a way that the witch knows that Christ became witchcraft and sorcery, so the manipulator knows that Christ became manipulation and wickedness and debauchery and perversion and abuse. God judged it all on Calvary so that I can preach the glorious Gospel of Jesus Christ and not exclude anybody. If God died for somebody, He died for everybody. Even if you despise what I have done in life, you cannot lock me out, because the same blood that covered your mess covered mine. Everything that we have ever done was placed on Him. Christ died on the Cross because He bore the iniquities of us all.

The Great Sin Bearer

So what happened to our sins? Two animals were used in the Old Testament sin offering, as described in Leviticus 16. One was a sacrificial lamb, which I have explained. But there was a second animal that is not mentioned as often—the scapegoat. "But the goat, on which the lot fell to be the scapegoat, shall be presented alive before the LORD, to make an atonement with him, and to let him go for a scapegoat into the wilderness" (Leviticus 16:10). The scapegoat was the one on which the priests symbolically laid the iniquities of Israel; then they slapped him, and he went running into the wilderness, carrying their sins away. The imagery is so strong that even in a secular setting, when someone ends up getting the ax for everyone else, we call that person a "scapegoat."

Thus Christ was not just my Sacrificial Lamb who paid the price for my sins. He was also the Scapegoat who carried my sins away.

The reason we have trouble getting today's church to enter into real worship, and the reason we have to pay so much to get all those pros to come in with all their high-powered instruments and all their vocal abilities to get us to supposedly enter into worship, is because we don't understand what Jesus did on the Cross. If we ever understand what Christ did for us, we won't ever need an organ or a drum set or a tambourine to worship God. When we know the goodness of Jesus on the Cross and all that He has done for us, our souls cannot help but cry out, "Hallelujah!"

When we don't understand what Jesus did, we end up praising God for stupid stuff. "Oh, praise God, I got a new car!" "Oh, they marked down that dress! Thank you, Jesus." "I got free tickets to the game! Bless

> *When we don't understand what Jesus did, we end up praising God for stupid stuff.*

the Lord." Meanwhile, God is looking at us as though we're crazy! What He provided for us is so much more than a dress, and it's so much more than a car! *When our soul was chained to the gates of hell, Jesus came Himself and died for us. When He took our sin upon Himself, He took our place and set us free!* If we are going to praise Him, we ought to praise Him for that! We ought to praise Jesus now!

What About You?

No One Too Wicked

If you think that you are too wicked and fallen for God to forgive you, I will tell you that I've seen witches and warlocks stumble down to the front of my church and receive God's full forgiveness and deliverance. The blood of Jesus did not back away from them! No, the blood said, "I'll cover that, too!"

God said, "If my people, which are called by my name, shall humble themselves, and pray, and seek my face, and turn from their wicked ways; then will I hear from heaven, and will forgive their sin, and will heal their land" (2 Chronicles 7:14). Whatever our sin, the blood of Jesus will wash it away. We can be clean! We can be healed!

Here's the truth: When Jesus died, He had us on His mind.

On His mind! The thing that the enemy is tormenting us with is guilt and shame. Jesus said, "I covered that, too!" It's as though He said, "Cast all your cares on Me, and let Me carry them away."

> *The thing that the enemy is tormenting us with is guilt and shame.*

Jesus is our Scapegoat. Remember when John the Baptist saw Jesus coming to him, and he said, "Behold the Lamb of God, which taketh away the sin of the world" (John 1:29). Throw your head back and cry out, "Take it away! Take away the guilt and the shame and the pain and the emotional dysfunction and all the collateral damage and all the side effects."

Face/Off

Years ago there was a movie that came out titled *Face/Off*. In the movie, a freelance terrorist has his face removed through surgery so that it can be reattached onto an FBI agent, which allows the agent to infiltrate the terrorist's network. The agent's face could also be removed and reattached onto the terrorist's face. The agent then was able to assume the identity of the evil terrorist, and vice versa. In our case, God has done a face/off. Jesus said, "I will cover your sin so well, I'm going to make you look like Me. So that when you go to the Father, don't use your name; but whatsoever you ask the Father in My name, He will do it for you!"

Salvation is a face/off. If you have been living life shame-faced, God says, "I have another face for you. I'll put it on you now! And just as I became evil for you, you will become righteous for Me." "For by grace are ye saved through faith; and that not of yourselves: it is the gift of God: Not of works, lest any man should boast" (Ephesians 2:8–9).

Whenever I preach or write about Calvary, it brings a whole different spirit into the room where I am. I feel the presence of the Lord, the kind of presence that brings real salvation—not just conviction, not just guilt, but real salvation, real deliverance. I feel a burning in my soul to minister to someone who needs a face/off, who needs to change places, who needs to be redeemed, who needs to be restored.

Jesus paid it all for us—all of it. But we won't receive it if we won't reach for it.

Come to Jesus.
It's as simple as that.
He is waiting on you.

This is the Gospel:
"God so loved the world,
that he gave his only begotten Son,
that whosoever believeth in him
should not perish,
but have everlasting life."

Come!

Where are you, Adam?
Where are you, Eve?
Where are you?

He paid for every sin!
He died in your place!
You were in His mind, too!

Come!

WHEN I SURVEY THE WONDROUS
CROSS ON WHICH THE PRINCE OF
GLORY DIED, MY RICHEST GAIN
I COUNT BUT LOSS, AND POUR
CONTEMPT ON ALL MY PRIDE.

SEE FROM HIS HEAD, HIS HANDS,
HIS FEET, SORROW AND LOVE
FLOW MINGLED DOWN! DID
E'ER SUCH LOVE AND SORROW
MEET, OR THORNS COMPOSE
SO RICH A CROWN?

WERE THE WHOLE REALM OF
NATURE MINE, THAT WERE A
PRESENT FAR TOO SMALL; LOVE SO
AMAZING, SO DIVINE, DEMANDS
MY SOUL, MY LIFE, MY ALL.

—Isaac Watts

THE CROSS— THE PLACE OF HIS PASSION

Many, many years ago, I read Acts 1:3, and it boggled my mind. At that moment, I couldn't understand why it had such an impact, because I had read it countless times and heard many people make reference to it. But reading it in the Word of God that day, it leaped out at me and birthed a message in my heart and in my spirit. I want you to read it in its context: "The former treatise have I made, O Theophilus, of all that Jesus began both to do and teach, until the day in which he was taken up, after that he through the Holy Ghost had given commandments unto the apostles whom he had chosen: to whom also he shewed himself alive after his passion by many infallible proofs, being seen of them forty days, and speaking of the things pertaining, to the kingdom of God" (Acts 1:1–3).

Luke states that Jesus "showed himself alive"—after what? "His passion!" As I read it, I was struck by the question: What is it about the Cross of Christ that when we see it, we see pain, but when God sees it, He sees passion? As I reflected on that thought, I was filled with amazement and wonder. It was as though I started to get my mind to wrap around the meaning of the passion of God. *How was it possible that God could love me like He did?*

I hope and trust that you'll get the same revelation as you read this chapter. It won't soak in totally as you read this for the first time. You've got to let the meaning of His passion marinate in your soul for a while. In this cold, loveless world, how could God love any of us when we are so indifferent and so difficult! I found myself repeating the questions, "God, You mean You love me like that? What do You see in me that is worthy of Your love? How can You call me beautiful when I know how rotten I am?"

If you are like I was, you have been going around trying to get others to love you as God loves you, and it's a search that leaves us empty and bitter. We can only find our fulfillment in God.

The Sheer Horror of the Cross

I am amazed by the pain and the agony and the torture of the Cross, the savage beating of His flesh, the stripping away of His privacy, the raw nudity of the Cross. Despite our artists' renditions of the Cross, there was no loincloth recorded in Scriptures. Jesus was stripped absolutely naked, nothing covering Him but blood from the beating of His brow and His back. The prophet Isaiah said, "There is no beauty that we should desire him" (Isaiah 53:2).

The Cross was a hideous place. I look at all the beautiful artistic depictions of handsome men with their arms stretched out on the Cross, looking calm and collected, with little droplets of blood falling down, and I realize none of them truly reflect the Cross. Jesus surely looked like He'd been on a butcher's block with ripped flesh and torn places in His body to the point He was not recognizable.

Perhaps what was depicted in the movie *The Passion* comes the closest to the real historical crucifixion. I actually watched the movie with Mel Gibson, who produced and directed the movie. I don't mean any disrespect to Gibson, but I saw it once and have no desire to see the DVD again. It's not as though you are getting ready to go out on a Friday night and say, "Hey, let's go see *The Passion* again." There's not been an evening since when I thought, *Hey, let's grill some steaks, fry some potatoes, and watch Jesus being beaten almost to death!* It was, from my perspective, painfully agonizing to watch. It was difficult to watch—at times I felt helpless, at times I felt angry, because I wanted to fight the guys who were beating Him. I just wanted to jump into the scene and attack!

You may have watched *The Passion* and wanted to worship. I was carnal; I wanted to fight! I was thinking, *If that creep hits Him one more time, I'm going to knock him out!* I'm sure that was not what Gibson intended me to get out of the movie, but that was my experience. I wanted to defend Jesus and help get Him out of there. Even now that's what's wrong with me—I want to help Jesus out of the horror of it, when He has made it clear that He had to do it *for* me.

> I want to help Jesus out of the horror of it, when He has made it clear that He had to do it for me.

Love Hurts

Luke records, "He shewed himself alive after his passion by many infallible proofs" (Acts 1:3). What is this coordination between His passion and pain that they are so hopelessly intertwined together? *Passion* and *pain*. The only people who dare have a glimpse at what I just said are lovers, because unless we have loved enough to discover the pain of passion, we are going to miss the essence of this message. To really understand, we have to have gone beyond the flutterings in our stomach and the goose pimples down our neck to discover for ourselves the utter discomfort of falling in love, the pain of loving another person. By the way, it doesn't even have to be a lover; it can be a child, a friend, or a parent.

The pain! How it hurts to be trapped in love! How we tell ourselves, "I am not going to feel this way! I am not going to let that person make a fool of me!" And yet we do it again and again! We do the very things we say we would never do, because love will lock us up in the incarceration of our emotions and leave us there! It is truly passion! It is great passion, but it is also great pain! Don't ever let anyone tell you love doesn't hurt. Love hurts!

It hurts to love!
It hurts to invest in people!
It hurts to be vulnerable!
It hurts to be that open!
It hurts to be that giving.

And the people who don't know the pain probably have not loved at a level to even begin to understand what I'm writing about.

Love is sacrificial.
Love is not self-serving.
Love is not puffed up.
Love does not behave itself unseemly.
Love does not seek its own.
Love makes us give someone our coat, and we walk home cold.
Love goes too far—it's overboard; it's across the track; it's over the line.

Love makes us love people who love the person we love, and it makes us fight people who fight the person we love. Love will make us get into a fight, and we might not even know what we are talking about, because we've got to defend the person we love because love is like that!

Knowing Love That Is Beyond Knowing

The apostle Paul's prayer for the Ephesians was: "That Christ may dwell in your hearts by faith; that ye, being rooted and grounded in love, may be able to comprehend with all saints what is the breadth, and length, and depth, and height; and to know the love of Christ, which passeth knowledge, that ye might be filled with all the fulness of God" (Ephesians 3:17–19). He prays that we would know the love of Christ, which is beyond knowing. To understand that, consider the many expressions of human love in your life, and you'll catch a glimpse. When I mention maternal love, you catch a glimpse of your mother's love. When I mention a best friend, you get a glimpse of his or her love.

But when I talk about the *agape* love of God, it is so difficult and intimidating to explain, because there is nothing that compares to divine love. Paul says it is unknowable, yet he tells us he wants us to know the unknowable; and though we cannot know it, we can sense it. And if we ever sense it, it will heal every aching place in our soul.

I believe with all my heart that this is what the psalmist David was talking about when he said, "Thou wilt shew me the path of life: in thy presence is fulness of joy; at thy right hand there are pleasures for evermore" (Psalm 16:11). I don't believe David was skipping and dancing and beating a tambourine when he wrote those words. This was more intimate than a dance. This was a place where divine love healed the hurts and achings in his soul. This was a place where David felt safe at last, because he has gone beyond the joy of serving God and the fascination of seeing God's power to the splendor of being a recipient of God's love. And in that place, if we can ever find it, there is fullness of joy, there is healing, and there is wholeness. But from Christ's perspective, in that place there is pain, because it hurts to love.

Created to Love

It wouldn't hurt so bad to love if we could pick the ones we love. Wouldn't it be easier if we interviewed people first? Do background checks. Personality profiles. Send any possible candidates for our love through a battery of tests. Or perhaps we should send them to a group of psychologists. Then, after they pass the rigorous tests and we've had a chance to thoroughly observe them for weeks, little by little we can inch into love,

> *It wouldn't hurt so bad to love if we could pick the ones we love.*

slowly and gradually. If we find that they are deserving and don't do anything crazy or come out of the bag acting as though they are bipolar or even tripolar, then maybe, just maybe, we can get something going with this love thing.

What is it about love that we stumble and fall into it? We don't plan it; it just happens. Sometimes we fall in love with someone at the same moment we are saying, "I don't want to!" Have you ever prayed not to feel how you feel? And then there's all the dumb stuff that we do, all the dumb stuff that we say, all the pet names we call each other, and the songs that we sing when we can't even sing! Have you ever had someone sing to you, even though they can't sing, but they are in love with you, so it's okay? Normally you would hang up the phone or want to put tape over their mouth, but now you think it's cute and wonderful because you are in love with them.

Have you ever loved someone who did not love you back? Everything in your commonsensical mind told you not to do it, but you did it. Even if you don't express it, you feel it; and there is something about love that wants to express itself. Feelings are not happy being locked up in jail. Feelings break loose and leave notes, give roses, or offer an extra goodie when we go through the school lunch line. "Here, you can have my cupcake!" Love will have to express itself in one way or another. How can something that is so strong make us feel so weak and cause us to do dumb stuff over and over again?

When God created man from the dust of the earth, He wanted something in His likeness, something in His image, something He could relate to, and something that could relate to Him (see Genesis 1:26–27). He also created man in His likeness because we like something that is like us. We want someone to love. And then we can have *koinonia,* or fellowship and communion, when we connect with others. There's intimacy, there's sharing in common, and there's love.

The Place of God's Passion

There are at least two places in Scripture where God gets very intimate with a person and shows them how He really feels. From my personal perspective, these are two times God crossed the line and stopped seeming like the sovereign God long enough to just sit down and be a guy and say, "Hey, man, let me tell you about what's going on with Me." One of the occasions occurred in His relationship with Abraham, and the other was with the prophet Hosea. We are going to look at them both in-depth, and it is all about the same thing— His passion. To Abraham, He shows "the place" of His passion, and to Hosea, He shows "the feeling" of His passion.

Let's look first at the incident with Abraham (Genesis 22:2–14, emphasis added) where God talks about "the place."

And [God] said, Take now thy son, thine only son Isaac, whom thou lovest, and get thee into the land of Moriah; and offer him there for a burnt offering upon one of the mountains which I will tell thee of.

*And Abraham rose up early in the morning, and saddled his ass, and took two of his young men with him, and Isaac his son, and clave the wood for the burnt offering, and rose up, and went unto **the place** of which God had told him. Then on the third day Abraham lifted up his eyes, and saw **the place** afar off. And Abraham said unto his young men, Abide ye here with the ass; and I and the lad will go yonder and worship, and come again to you.*

And Abraham took the wood of the burnt offering, and laid it upon Isaac his son; and he took the fire in his hand, and a knife; and they went both of them together.

And Isaac spake unto Abraham his father, and said, My father: and he said, Here am I, my son. And he said, Behold the fire and the wood: but where is the lamb for a burnt offering?

And Abraham said, My son, God will provide himself a lamb for a burnt offering: so they went both of them together.

*And they came to **the place** which God had told him of; and Abraham built an altar there, and laid the wood* *in order, and bound Isaac his son, and laid him on the altar upon the wood. And Abraham stretched forth his hand, and took the knife to slay his son. And the angel of the LORD called unto him out of heaven, and said, Abraham, Abraham: and he said, Here am I.*

And he said, Lay not thine hand upon the lad, neither do thou any thing unto him: for now I know that thou fearest God, seeing thou hast not withheld thy son, thine only son from me.

And Abraham lifted up his eyes, and looked, and behold behind him a ram caught in a thicket by his horns: and Abraham went and took the ram, and offered him up for a burnt offering in the stead of his son. And Abraham called the name of that place Jehovahjireh: as it is said to this day, In the mount of the LORD it shall be seen.

God opened up His heart to Abraham and said, "I want you to see what it is like to take your son, your only son, and offer his life up as a sacrifice. I didn't want you to really kill him, but to take him as if you are going to offer him up. But, first, I wanted you to experience the journey to expose you to *the place* where I'll one day bring My own Son to die as the Sacrificial Lamb. Second, I wanted your experience to connect you with the feeling of how much it cost Me to love you like this. Abraham, take your boy, your only child, and raise your knife as if to slay him, and then you will begin to understand what Calvary was to Me, how much it cost Me."

Incidentally, when Abraham came to *the place* on Mount Moriah where he offered up his son Isaac, it was on that same mount that we have Calvary, the place of Jesus' passion. Abraham saw the cost of His passion, and it no doubt shaped the rest of his life. How could it not?

> "*Abraham, take your boy, your only child, and raise your knife as if to slay him. Only then will you begin to understand what Calvary was to Me, how much it cost Me.*"

But when it comes to the passion of the Cross, God does not let Abraham feel the gross weight of His passion. No, He saves that for a guy named Hosea—a nice, neat little Jewish prophet who has saved himself for marriage and kept himself untainted from the world. God says to the prophet, "Hosea, I want you to really connect with My pulse speed. I want you to understand My passion. I want you to know what it is like for Me to love the people of Israel."

Being the fine prophet he was, Hosea responded, "Yes, Lord, speak to me. I am your prophet. I am your servant. I'm ready to go. What is it?"

And God said, "Go, take unto thee a wife of whoredoms and children of whoredoms: for the land hath committed great whoredom, departing from the LORD" (Hosea 1:2). Can you imagine how difficult that must have been? What must it have been like to think that your marriage to a prostitute, which everyone is going to find out about, is going to be used as a symbol of the relationship of God and Israel? The prophet of God is to marry a common prostitute.

As rough as that was for starters, if you read the rest of the first chapter of Hosea, you find that Hosea takes Gomer as his wife, and they have three children. But after the three children were born, Gomer once again took to the streets and her prostituting. At that point, we can imagine Hosea saying, "Okay, I gave this marriage thing a test drive, and it's over. She's abandoned me and the children and is living in the gutter. God, I did what You asked me to do. I have three lovely children to care for, and I abhor what my wife is doing. I get it—I understand Your heart and how You hate Israel's sin. I appreciate what You've taught me, and I'll declare it across the nation. Now let's get the divorce papers together and end this mess."

However, that is not what God told Hosea to do, despite how despicably Gomer was living in sin. "Then said the LORD unto me, Go yet, love a woman beloved of her friend, yet an adulteress, according to the love of the LORD toward the children of Israel, who look to other gods, and love flagons of wine" (Hosea 3:1). God is saying to Hosea, "No, there's more to this than going through with a marriage ceremony and making some children. I want you to feel My passion, My love. I want you to fall in love with her, even though she's rejected you and is sleeping with anyone who will pay her."

It's possible that you know what that is like. It's possible that you are going through a similar situation right now. You don't have to be single to go through rejection and doubt. You can be married and have passion for someone who is not in love with you. You know something of the heart of God as regards His love for us, because you're doing the same.

So Hosea went out and stood on the corner of the red-light district, and he looked and he waited and he waited and he saw her and he loved her. He loved her at a distance. He didn't know how much hard work love was; he just loved her. He didn't know the details or the depth of the dysfunction; he just loved her. She had her hair done up and all of the adornments and degradation that go along with her prostitution, but Hosea didn't see her as others saw her. He saw something in her that no one else could see or cared to see.

Herein lies the difficulty of love. This is why our friends can't tell us anything when we fall in love, and this is why we don't listen to our mothers. This is why we will fight off our own brothers and sisters and tell them they are crazy and that they never thought the one we love was anything. They just can't see the good in our love because love is blind.

Hosea loved her and said to himself, "Surely, if I love her, and if I am good to her, and if I treat her better than she has ever been treated, there will be reciprocity." You don't have to be a bad person to have a bad relationship. You can even be a prophet of God and have a bad relationship. You can do all the right things in all the right ways and say all the right words and give yourself unabashedly and unashamedly and still not get the reciprocity you need to maintain the tenacity of love. Have you ever loved and not received it back—at least not in the same fashion, not to the same degree? Maybe you got a few droppings here and there, but it was not coming back to you with the same intensity of your love?

Being a very intense person myself, I can tell you that a great frustration of life is when you are an intense person and you love someone who is not intense. Have you ever been intense when the other person was indifferent? Have you ever been intense and the other person was casual? You love them at a level ten, and they respond on a level two. The frustration drives you crazy, and you complain about it and say you are not going through it, but you do go through it again because you are a ten in love with a two. I think all the twos should get together, and all the tens should get together, and we wouldn't have this craziness!

When you love like a ten and fall in love with someone who loves like a two, then comes the pain. The pain is the emptiness you feel from the lack of response, because there is nothing as deflating as a poor response. Let's say that you are a detailed person and want everything to be just right, and you have so much love and care to give the other person and know how to express it creatively, but you have fallen in love with someone who is noncommunicative and unexpressive and not thoughtful. At first, you don't notice it, because you're so in love; but after a while, even you have to open your eyes enough to see that there is an inequity in the relationship.

When Love Is Not Reciprocated

God expresses the inequity in His relationship with the children of Israel through the inequity expressed in the relationship between the prophet and the prostitute. He is

> *I am to you what the prophet is, and you are to Me what the prostitute is. To you, it's just a product; but to Me, it's a relationship.*

saying, "That is how unequally yoked you and I are. I am to you what the prophet is, and you are to Me what the prostitute is. To you, it's just a product; but to Me, it's a relationship."

If you are not familiar with the story, Hosea loved Gomer openly. It is one thing to love secretly, but it is another thing when love goes public. It's one thing to be a secret admirer—at least you can keep your pride and dignity. But what do you do when your love goes public and your woman is openly running around with every man who will pay for time with her?

I'm a guy, and I know how guys talk to one another about a woman who has been around. "Look, man, I know you're a nice guy, but she's not the one. Now, I don't want to get in your business, but she's not the one. You know, I'm not going to say nothin' about her, but she's been around with the fellas a little bit. I'm not saying you can't see her or somethin', but all that stuff you're doin'—getting her a car, getting her an apartment—look, she gave me her phone number last night. You know what I'm sayin'?"

Love is embarrassing when it is not reciprocated. It messes up our other relationships. There is collateral damage when it is not reciprocated, because people who love us hate to see us go through the pain of our passion. They try to save us because of our pain, and we fight them because of our passion. There is conflict.

God said, "Loving Israel is making a huge conflict for me. So, Hosea, you go down there and marry a tramp, so you can see what I am going through loving My people. While I love you, you are looking somewhere else."

Hosea took her and gave her everything she could have ever wanted. Everything she was out there working the street for, he gave it to her. He brought her into his house, and he gave her everything, but he could not change her mentality. Sometimes God's goodness will take us to a place where we cannot rest, because we are hooked on evil and iniquity; and even though He offered us a better life, it didn't taste good to us because we have been hooked on trash. There is nothing more difficult than for a good man to offer himself and all he has to a woman who loves bad boys. He ends up being a brother figure to her. He picks her up after some bum hits her in the head with a pipe wrench, and he cleans her up; and she says she is never going back to her lover, and that makes him glad, because he wants to be with her. The next thing he knows, she is back with the creep again; he is mad enough to kill her, but he can't because he loves her, and he is trapped.

Love put God in a trap!

Love Redeems

So Hosea brought her into his house and took care of her. He cherished her; but she kept slipping out, doing what she was, because ultimately people do what they are. And you think he would stop loving her, even though she actually went down from being a harlot to being a slave. Hosea went out looking for her, but he could not find her, and she did not come back. He searched high and low, but he could not find Gomer. "Have you seen her? Have you seen Gomer? Have you seen my wife? I'm looking for Gomer. If you see my wife, would you tell her I'm looking for her?"

Hosea was looking for her down at the market, and he saw her! Tragically, she was stripped naked on a slave table. All the men were gawking at her, looking her up and down, checking her out like a piece of meat. Anybody else would have said, "That's it!" and walked away. But Hosea took out his money and said, "Don't sell her yet. I'm getting my money together!" He fumbled with his money. His friends came up to him and tried to prevent this transaction, but he said, "No, I have to get her back!" He saw her clothing lying all tattered on the ground, and he was in anguish. "You just don't know, man. I've got to get her back. She is beautiful to me. I love her. She is beautiful to me."

"So I bought her to me for fifteen pieces of silver, and for an homer of barley, and an half homer of barley" (Hosea 3:2). This is the most important part for you to see: If anybody else at the market had purchased Gomer, it would have been a fair transaction; but Hosea was buying his own wife. He was buying his own bride off a slave table. She wouldn't stop cheating, and he had to pay the price of reconciliation to redeem her. He purchased her from the spot she should never have been in the first place, because he loved her to the degree of helplessness. He did this all to buy her back.

My point is to express the passion that God has for Israel, even after Israel has repeatedly played the harlot with Him. This is how He expressed it within the context of the story of Hosea and Gomer in Hosea 2:14–23:

Therefore, behold, I will allure her, and bring her into the wilderness, and speak comfortably unto her. And I will give her her vineyards from thence, and the valley of Achor for a door of hope: and she shall sing there, as in the days of her youth, and as in the day when she came up out of the land of Egypt.

And it shall be at that day, saith the LORD, that thou shalt call me Ishi; and shalt call me no more Baali. For I will take away the names of Baalim out of her mouth, and they shall no more be remembered by their name. And in that day will I make a covenant for them with the beasts of the field and with the fowls of heaven, and with the creeping things of the ground: and I will break the bow and the sword and the battle out of the earth, and will make them to lie down safely. And I will betroth thee unto me for ever; yea, I will betroth thee unto me in righteousness, and in judgment, and in lovingkindness, and in mercies. I will even betroth thee unto me in faithfulness: and thou shalt know the LORD.

And it shall come to pass in that day, I will hear, saith the LORD, I will hear the heavens, and they shall hear the earth; and the earth shall hear the corn, and the wine, and the oil; and they shall hear Jezreel. And I will sow her unto me in the earth; and I will have mercy upon her that had not obtained mercy; and I will say to them which were not my people, Thou art my people; and they shall say, Thou art my God.

Do you hear the passion in God's voice? Do you see the love of the God who "so loved the world, that He gave His only begotten Son"? It's not that He loved—He *so loved* that He paid for something that should have been His in the first place, and in leaving Him had been horribly defiled. We get ourselves into the same forsaken place—sold as slaves to sin! He has to go get us from that place.

> He said to those who were gawking at her nakedness, "She is not like the others. I have chosen her!"

When Hosea got her from that place, he covered her nakedness and smoothed her hair back and caressed her face and said, "It's okay, it's okay. You never really loved me like you should have loved me, but I never stopped loving you. Come on, let's go home." And he said to those who were gawking at her nakedness, "She is not like the others. I have chosen her! I don't know what you are going to do with the others, but you cannot have this one. She is mine. I don't want to hear what she has done. She is my chosen one!"

The Passion of the Cross

This is the place of passion and the place of pain. Jesus comes to buy us back and redeem us! While others scoff and jeer, He says, "I want to get you out of this." If you've ever been in a mess and disgraced and humiliated God, and if God has ever had to come where you are and get you out of your mess, He certainly said to you, "I still love you. I still love you! I'm going to wipe away those tears! Come here, baby. I'm going to wash away the filth and cover you with My righteousness. I'm going to give you your name back. I'm going to give you your dignity back. I'm going to restore to you all that the world has taken from you. Come here!"

We think Calvary was about pain? It was about passion! It was about a God who had everything and fell in love with a soul who had nothing—no morals, no dignity, no standards, no class—but God was willing to do anything, anytime and anyplace. "But where sin abounded, grace did much more abound" (Romans 5:20). Hallelujah, O my soul!

Jesus said, "Sit here. I'm going to restore you. I'm going to fill you. I'm going to love you. I'm going to give you My name. I'm not going to just be your 'Baali' or 'master,' but I'm going to be 'Ishi,' for I'm going to be your husband!" And He says, "Because I love you, I'm going to open doors for you. You know that job you got? That was Me! And when your credit was messed up, I was the one who opened the doors so you got that car anyway. And when they set a trap for you and tried to destroy you, but someone intervened and helped you just in the nick of time—that was Me! Because I fight battles for you; I open doors for you. I made a way for you. When you didn't even have a job, I fed you! I knew you were sleeping around, and I knew you were messing around. I knew, but I loved you!

> I am here to tell you that Jesus loves you like that!
> He loves you over the top of every obstacle, over every problem, over every mistake.
> He loves you with crazy grace, even when He smells the scent of unfaithfulness on you!
> He knows about those abortions, and He still loves you!
> He knows about the gay affair, and He still loves you!
> He knows about your cheating with that money, and He still loves you!
> He was loving you when you were in jail, and He was loving you through all your diseases.
> He was loving you through all your mistakes, for this is the Gospel.

This is Calvary's message. This is why the Romans hung Jesus high and stretched Him wide. "He was wounded for our transgressions, he was bruised for our iniquities: the chastisement of our peace was upon him; and with his stripes we are healed" (Isaiah 53:5). "The chastisement of our peace was upon Him" means He was beaten so you could sleep at night.

He was beaten so you could live with your unlivable past. He was beaten so you could laugh, because He heard you say, "I don't think I will ever smile again." He paid the price to put the smile back on your face. He paid the price to put the skip back in your walk. He paid the price to put the joy back in your life again. This is the Gospel.

So the next time you see a Cross, see the passion of the divine Lover. The next time you see blood, see the price that He paid for your redemption. He died for your deliverance!

God Has a Place for You

I hear women today complain because the Bible says, "Wives, submit yourselves unto your own husbands, as unto the Lord" (Ephesians 5:22). I honestly don't feel sorry for them, because the man has the tougher role. "Husbands, love your wives, even as Christ also loved the church, and gave himself for it" (Ephesians 5:25). How can a guy like me be expected to do a thing like that? We are to love our wives in the same manner that Christ gave Himself? That means we don't always get to be

> How can a guy like me be expected to do a thing like that? We are to love our wives in the same manner that Christ gave Himself?

happy, and we don't always get everything we want, and our relationship isn't always going to be fair, because we are to love our wives as Christ loved the church, and love isn't fair!

Do you know why this is the hardest message that I will ever teach or preach? It's because we know so little about being loved. The idea escapes us because it is so seldom lived out in real life. When Paul tells husbands to love their wives as Christ loved the church, he uses marriage as a metaphor. He is saying that what we need to understand is that the marriage between a man and woman is a picture of Christ and the church. In that picture, Christ is the negative and the church is the photo. The question is, if you mess with the negative, what does that say about the photo? Most marriages are not a picture of Christ and His church. If we ever loved others as Christ loves, half of the healing lines in church would disappear, whole wings of hospitals would close down, and psychiatrists and psychologists would go out of business. If we truly knew how much Christ loved us, our world would change.

Hosea brought Gomer to a safe, loving place from which she kept sneaking away. He kept buying her back and bringing her back to the place. She wasn't sneaking away because of her past; she snuck away because she did not believe in her future. When our past impulse is stronger than our future perception, and then trouble breaks out, we will always revert back to the familiar. Even if the familiar is abusive, we keep going back to it.

Perhaps you are all too familiar with Gomer's actions? God keeps pulling you out of your mess, but you keep going back to your past. And you go back to it, not because you are happy with it; you go back to it because you are used to it.

If you enter into His passion, He will deliver you from your mess.

If all you have ever experienced is *religion*, the Cross is merely a religious symbol. I say to you that the Cross is the place of relationship. You say it was pain; Jesus called it passion. If you enter into His passion, He will deliver you from your mess.

Take a few moments and reflect on your life. Can you imagine a God who knows your deepest, darkest secrets and yet keeps saying, "You are so beautiful to Me. You are my chosen"? I realize how hard it is to receive that kind of love when you've done some nasty, dirty stuff. You don't feel worthy of love, so you reject it. Sometimes you go back to the abuse because you feel you deserve it.

From the Cross, Christ cried out, "I thirst!" But it wasn't for water. It was for you! Two thousand years later, He says, "I'm waiting for you! I have a place for you. I have a life for you. I have joy for you. I have gifts for you. I see you with the Lover of your soul. I'm waiting." The Lover of your soul, from a rugged Cross, from a place of untold pain and agony and passion, says, "I love you still! I love you still!"

I know a lot of people, especially men, who come to church and look fine and act secure, but they are closed to all of the amazing and passionate potential that their life holds, because they've never opened their hearts. Jesus says, "I'm waiting! I already know how wonderful you will be!"

I believe that heaven will be a place where all pain is turned to passion, all our searches will end, and life will truly begin. I went to God and told Him that, and He said, "You don't have to wait until you get there! If you come closer to Me, you can have it right now."

God has a place for you. You can go to church till you are blue in the face, but if you do not open your heart, you are going to miss it! I can feel Him wooing you! God has a gift for you; and like any gift, you can throw it away, you can play with it, you can say that there's nothing to this, or you can receive it and use it. Something is missing in your life that God wants to fill.

This is what Calvary is all about. Money will not get you out of what you are in, because Jesus did not redeem you with money! He redeemed you with His blood. I could be more theological in how I state this, but *God wants you.*

If your mouth is dry for Jesus,
if there is a thirst in your soul
for His love,
if there is a longing in your spirit
for His grace,
if you don't care
what other people think or say,
if your heart aches for Him,
and you want Him,
you want Him,
you want Him,
you really want Him,

Come to Jesus.
He is waiting for you!

THERE HE STANDS ARRAYED IN
HUMAN FLESH; HIS CROSS IS HIS
ALTAR, HIS BODY AND HIS SOUL THE
VICTIM, HIMSELF THE PRIEST. AND
LO! BEFORE HIS GOD HE OFFERS UP
HIS OWN SOUL WITHIN THE VEIL
OF THICK DARKNESS THAT HAS
COVERED HIM FROM THE SIGHT
OF MEN. PRESENTING HIS OWN
BLOOD, HE ENTERS WITHIN THE
VEIL, SPRINKLES IT THERE, AND
COMING FORTH FROM THE MIDST
OF THE DARKNESS, HE LOOKS DOWN
ON THE ASTONISHED EARTH AND
UPWARD TO EXPECTANT HEAVEN
AND CRIES, "IT IS FINISHED!"

—*Charles Spurgeon*

Chapter 5

THE PLOT OF
THE PRIEST

If I were to give you a quiz about what we've covered so far in this book, I hope you are able to recount the lessons that will help take you from the Cross to Pentecost. Each teaching is a step on our way to the fullness of the Holy Spirit.

1. We've learned that mankind's access to the tree of life was denied because of Adam's choice to turn his back on a relationship with his loving Creator. We've also learned that the bloody coats of skins that covered Adam and Eve's nakedness were a substitution for greater things to come through Christ.
2. We've learned that through the Cross, God has restored access to His presence and that we can come boldly to the throne of grace.

3. We've learned that the Cross was a symbol of evil; inasmuch as Christ who knew no sin became sin for us. We've learned that Jesus was the scapegoat who takes away the sins of the world that we might be forgiven and free.

4. We've learned about the passion required for Christ to die for us on the Cross and that we can have a life and a relationship with Him that is absolutely mind-boggling.

How do we know when we've learned these lessons? Jesus said, "Ye shall know the truth, and the truth shall make you free" (John 8:32). As we learn these teachings, the burden of guilt and shame and abuse and trauma and drugs and perversion is lifted off our shoulders. The more we learn about how Christ liberated us through the Cross, the more we walk in the freedom of being sons and daughters of God. We get so bold that we are unafraid to tell the devil to back away, because of who we are in Christ Jesus and what He has done for us. We start shouting "Glory to God!" because Jehovah Jireh has provided a perfect provision for us—Jesus Christ the Righteous One.

As we go deeper still into the Word of God, it is my intention to show you the way from the Cross to Pentecost. The Cross embodies in the New Testament what the Passover was in the Old Testament. You cannot have Pentecost without Passover, because Pentecost is fifty days after the Passover in the Jewish calendar. Pentecost sets its watch by the Passover. It is meaningless to talk about God filling us with His Spirit (Pentecost) if we haven't been washed in Jesus' blood (Passover). Once you have received Him as your Savior and Lord and been washed in the blood of the Lamb, you have the

> *It is meaningless to talk about God filling us with His Holy Spirit (Pentecost) if we haven't been washed in Jesus' blood (Passover).*

right to expect and experience the privileges and benefits that go along with being a child of the Most High God!

My intent in this chapter is to bring a clear revelation of what happened on the Cross, lest we minimize that which is the hinge between the Old Testament law and New Testament grace. Without the Cross, the door cannot open. The Cross is the hinge that connects the Jew to the Gentile. The Cross is the hinge between justice and mercy, between death and life, and between curses and blessings. The Cross is the hinge that opens the door to the love of God.

Whenever I write or speak on the Cross, I know I'm on holy ground. As we near the Cross, I find that God's people fall back in love with Jesus in a fresh way. Our relationship with God is similar to our relationship in marriage. Husbands and wives don't love each other with the same passion all the time. We have periods of falling in and out of love, seasons of lesser and greater passion. Some couples will have a low season and walk away from each other. As it is in the natural world, so it is with the spiritual. There are times when we are more on fire for God than we are at other times. It is not every day when we are in the spiritual honeymoon suite, locked up with the Bridegroom, throwing kisses, eating chocolate-covered strawberries, and sipping a little bubbly on the side.

Expect this chapter to be more intense; expect me to engage your focus and thinking in deeper biblical waters. This is not a spectator sport or a movie in which you sit and watch passively. This is an opportunity for you to enter into a deeper understanding and revelation of what the Cross means, how it happened, and how it affects us today.

The Miracle That Led to the Cross

To understand the background for this teaching, I'm asking you to stop a moment, open your Bible, and read John 11. It is the familiar biblical story of the death and resurrection of

Jesus' friend Lazarus, who lived at Bethany with his sisters, Mary and Martha. Jesus knew that Lazarus was sick, and He could have gotten to Lazarus in time to heal him. Yet He purposely stayed away and allowed Lazarus to get worse and worse and finally to die, because Lazarus was critical in the plan of God. Jesus purposely held back until Lazarus died, then woke him up from the dead, because this crisis was the catalyst for Christ to expose His power in their lives.

If you are in a crisis or difficult place right now, highlight this point: The crisis is the catalyst for Christ to expose His power in your life! When God is ready to expose His power, He releases it through a crisis, for "God is our refuge and strength, a very present help in trouble" (Psalm 46:1). But if you avoid the trouble, you avoid Him, because Jesus says, "My strength is made perfect in weakness" (2 Corinthians 12:9).

Jesus allowed the circumstances to mount and the tension to build until Lazarus died. Interestingly, people don't come when someone is sick; but when that person dies, everyone comes rushing to see. And into this mass gathering of witnesses, Jesus comes to give them a demonstration of His resurrection power in John 11:43–57.

> *And when he thus had spoken, he cried with a loud voice, Lazarus, come forth. And he that was dead came forth,*

bound hand and foot with graveclothes: and his face was bound about with a napkin.

Jesus saith unto them, Loose him, and let him go.

Then many of the Jews which came to Mary, and had seen the things which Jesus did, believed on him. But some of them went their ways to the Pharisees, and told them what things Jesus had done.

Then gathered the chief priests and the Pharisees a council, and said, What do we? for this man doeth many miracles. If we let him thus alone, all men will believe on him: and the Romans shall come and take away both our place and nation.

And one of them, named Caiaphas, being the high priest that same year, said unto them, Ye know nothing at all, nor consider that it is expedient for us, that one man should die for the people, and that the whole nation perish not.

And this spake he not of himself: but being high priest that year, he prophesied that Jesus should die for that nation; and not for that nation only, but that also he should gather together in one the children of God that were scattered abroad. Then from that day forth they took counsel together for to put him to death.

Jesus therefore walked no more openly among the Jews; but went thence unto a country near to the wilderness, into a city called Ephraim, and there continued with his disciples.

And the Jews' passover was nigh at hand: and many went out of the country up to Jerusalem before the passover, to purify themselves. Then sought they for Jesus, *and spake among themselves, as they stood in the temple, What think ye, that he will not come to the feast? Now both the chief priests and the Pharisees had given a commandment, that, if any man knew where he were, he should shew it, that they might take him.*

Lazarus, who had been in the grave for four days, came forth bound hand and foot. He came forth by the command of Jesus, and our focus goes to the diverse reaction of the crowd. Because of the audacity of Lazarus' resurrection, we can get so caught up in the miracle that we miss the atmosphere in which it took place. I want us to notice this specifically because it is parallel to what often happens in our own lives. Sometimes God is blessing us, and we are so caught up in the blessing that we don't see in the periphery that there are those who are glad for us and there are those who are not glad for us.

Jesus had just raised Lazarus from the dead, and some people were shouting and rejoicing. No doubt Mary and Martha were weeping for joy, and it states that many of the Jews believed in Jesus. Wouldn't you believe? If you

> *Wouldn't you believe, if you saw a dead man who had been stinking in the grave for four days come out and take a sip of coffee?*

saw a dead man who had been stinking in the grave for four days come out and take a sip of coffee, wouldn't you believe? If I started to raise folks from the dead in my church, I would hope that the membership would increase exponentially! But then again, I'm not sure. Not everyone was jumping up and down for joy that day.

Not far away there was another group at the edge of the crowd who "went their ways to the Pharisees, and told them what things Jesus had done. Then gathered the chief priests and the Pharisees a council, and said, What do we? for this man doeth many miracles. If we let him thus alone, all men will believe on him: and the Romans shall come and take away both our place and nation." Some who watched the miracle also hated Jesus for His power and influence and were determined to stop Him.

The same is true today. The more powerful and influential people become, the more hated they will be. It's true no matter what you do in life.

It is amazing to me that leaders often get into more trouble from their associates than from their known enemies. Dr. Martin Luther King Jr. is lauded as one of the great leaders for minorities in the 1960s, and you can hardly go into a large city in this country today that does not have a Martin

Luther King Boulevard. But many of the churches that honor him today hated and rejected him when he was alive, refusing to allow him to speak and putting him out of their conventions and organizations.

Martin Luther, who was the catalyst for the Protestant Reformation in the 1500s, restored the teaching of justification by faith to the church, nailing his *Ninety-Five Theses* on the door of the Roman Catholic Church. And through that nail hole, the grace of God escaped to broaden its capacity and reach a broader dimension of people around the world. Luther is now lauded as one of the greatest Christian leaders, but in his day he was condemned as a heretic.

Understand this: If you are not willing to deal with criticism, you cannot be Christ's disciple. You simply must expect that there will be a certain amount of cynicism that will go along with what God has told you to do. Jesus said, "If the world hates you, you know that it hated Me before it hated you" (John 15:18).

But I want to draw your attention to the fact that the hate toward Christ was coming from the religious folk. It was the chief priests and Pharisees who called a council meeting and said, "We need to do something about Jesus! If we don't stop Him the whole world is going to go after Him. If we don't do something to stop Him, Rome is going to attack us for His effectiveness."

Now focus on the words of Caiaphas, the high priest. "Ye know nothing at all, nor consider that it is expedient for us, that one man should die for the people, and that the whole nation perish not." In other words, "It is better for one to die for all than for all to die." It is important to understand that these are the words of the high priest, because although he is a cynic and impure in his attitude toward God, it is the catalyst of his statement that takes the Cross from being a place of execution to a place of a sin offering. Let's go even deeper!

Remember that Jesus was not the first or the last person to be crucified. Crucifixion in the Roman Empire was the equivalent of today's electric chair or gas chamber or lethal injection. It was the chosen method that the Romans had perfected to execute criminals. Even on the day that Jesus died, He was not crucified alone. So why do we worship Him and honor His Cross and ignore the others? It is because the other men were executed, but Christ was offered up as a sacrifice! But the Romans could not offer up a sacrifice to a God whom they did not worship. It had to come from Caiaphas, because it was written in the Jewish law that only a priest could legitimately offer up a sacrifice unto God for the people.

Even though Caiaphas's motives were still a necessary component in the process, for if Pilate crucified Jesus without Caiaphas's consent, it would have been a mere execution. The power of His Cross would have

> *If Pilate crucified Jesus without Caiaphas's consent, it would have been a mere execution.*

been no greater than the others who died alongside Him that day.

But because the crucifixion started with the high priest and not a politician, it is an offering and not an execution! When Caiaphas opened his mouth to speak against Jesus and said He had to be offered up, he unknowingly and unwittingly moved Jesus' agenda further along. "And this spake he not of himself: but being high priest that year, he prophesied that Jesus should die for that nation."

Now we understand why Lazarus had to die! It was all a setup to strategically activate a domino effect, a sequence of events.

If Lazarus had not gotten sick, he wouldn't have died then.
If Lazarus had not died then, the crowd wouldn't have gathered.

If Lazarus had not died, Jesus wouldn't have raised
him up.

If Jesus had not raised him up, then those "many
Jews" would not have believed in Christ.

If Jesus had not raised him up, jealousy would not
have broken out among the Jews and Caiaphas,
and there never would have been a meeting and
a decision by the high priest that would take the
death of Christ from being an execution to an offering.

God will allow certain things to happen in our lives that
we don't understand when it happens, but He will use it for
His purpose. I'm talking about negative things—about things
that make us weak, about things that wrench our hearts and
tear at our guts. I mean things that make us cry, "This is not
fair, this is not right!" Know that our God is a strategist; He
moves by methodology. God has structure and order, and
when something crazy happens and it makes no sense, it is
a sign that in the bigger scheme of things, "All things work
together for good to those who love God, to those who are
the called according to *His* purpose" (Romans 8:28, emphasis
mine).

The Instrumentality of the High Priest

Caiaphas was the current high priest. As the high priest, he had not only religious significance but influence among the decision makers to start a plot in motion for which we often give Judas ultimate credit. But Judas was just a pawn in the hand of destiny. Recognizing this is important, because we often spend time wrestling with or obsessing over our enemies, not recognizing that they can do to us only what God allows them to do. Rather than fighting them, we can walk up to them, shake them by the hand, and say, "You know what? It was good that I was afflicted for if I had not been afflicted, I would never have known the power of God."

As Caiaphas began to broach the subject that set in motion a plot to bring about the demise of Christ, he was unknowingly playing right into the purpose of God. He thought his plot was a decision for the betterment of the Jews in general, but he didn't know that God was using him and even his animosity.

As we read about the events surrounding Jesus' crucifixion, there was a jockeying back and forth between the Roman Empire and the Jewish religious community. If you're not aware of the history of Israel, the Romans had taken control over Jerusalem. Rome had a massive empire, and the Jews were under the sovereign power of Caesar. Pontius Pilate was one of Caesar's subordinate leaders, and it was his job to run and control the affairs of Israel. The Romans did not embrace the idea of a monotheistic God, such as Jehovah, as the only one true and living God. Theirs was a polytheistic religion that included all types of gods over all types of things. So if the Romans had offered up Christ, their involvement or instrumentality in it would have defiled Him. It had to come from His own people, from those who believed in God and the Messiah.

Watch this! Now I am taking you to John 18:13–28, where Jesus has been arrested. We are viewing the questioning of Jesus by the high priest that led to the crucifixion. And I want you to see what is going on from Caiaphas's perspective. For the sake of that focus, I have taken out the verses that regard Peter's betrayal.

> *And led him away to Annas first; for he was father in law to Caiaphas, which was the high priest that same year. Now Caiaphas was he, which gave counsel to the Jews, that it was expedient that one man should die for the people. . . . The high priest then asked Jesus of his disciples, and of his doctrine.*

Jesus answered him, I spake openly to the world; I ever taught in the synagogue, and in the temple, whither the Jews always resort; and in secret have I said nothing. Why askest thou me? ask them which heard me, what I have said unto them: behold, they know what I said.

And when he had thus spoken, one of the officers which stood by struck Jesus with the palm of his hand, saying, Answerest thou the high priest so?

Jesus answered him, If I have spoken evil, bear witness of the evil: but if well, why smitest thou me?

Now Annas had sent him bound unto Caiaphas the high priest. . . .

Then led they Jesus from Caiaphas unto the hall of judgment: and it was early; and they themselves went not into the judgment hall, lest they should be defiled; but that they might eat the passover.

Notice this was the high priest, not the Roman government, who was questioning Jesus. They had brought Him through due process of their law to the high priest before they took him to Pontius Pilate. Annas had previously been an acting high priest, and by Jewish law the high priesthood was held for life (Numbers 3:10). It is thought that Annas was the president of the Sanhedrin, or deputy or coadjutor of the high priest, and thus also called and legally considered high priest along with Caiaphas (Luke 3:2). For our purposes, it is important to note that the Jewish high priest set the plot into motion against Jesus and also is the one judging whether Christ should live or die.

After questioning Jesus, Annas sent Him bound to Caiaphas the high priest. If you are a student of the Bible, you know that Christ is the sacrifice and that the sacrifice must be tied to the altar. It was expedient that they brought Jesus to the high priest "bound," because this is a reflection of what occurred in the Old Testament when the priest would take a sacrifice and secure it on the altar so that it might be offered up.

In our own lives, this means that even our bondages have a purpose with God. Sometimes God won't let us move, He allows us to be tied up, because He is going to get some glory out of our affliction. "I can't move the way I want to move, Lord." "I can't afford what I used to be able to afford, Lord." "I don't have the help the way I would like to, Lord." That's all right! The bondages are in the plot not to hinder our lives, but for the complete realization of our lives.

> *This means that even our bondages have a purpose with God.*

Let's go deeper into this. Jesus was then led to Pontius Pilate and "the hall of judgment," where His trial would take place. The judgment hall was so corrupt that the priests would not go in there. That is why the decision had to be made by the high priest outside the judgment hall, so that Christ could present Himself effectively for the sins of the world.

If you continue to read in John 18, you see that Pilate was sitting on the judgment seat with Jesus standing before him. In the midst of Pilate's interview with Jesus, his wife sends him this message: "Have thou nothing to do with that just man: for I have suffered many things this day in a dream because of him" (Matthew 27:19). Pilate had already been trying to find a way to turn Jesus loose, because he considered Jesus innocent of the charges. The reason his wife had the dream was to push and make certain that Pilate's hands would not be on Christ.

In Matthew 27, we see Pilate desperately trying to get out of being involved in killing an innocent man. He offered to release one prisoner, which was often done during the Passover celebration, but the crowd chose Barabbas over Jesus. Note this point: "The chief priests and elders persuaded the multitude that they should ask Barabbas, and destroy Jesus" (v. 20). When asked by Pilate what should be done with Jesus, they shouted, "Crucify Him!" If the chief priests had not given their assent, it would not have been a sacrifice.

Further, "When Pilate saw that he could prevail nothing, but that rather a tumult was made, he took water, and washed his hands before the multitude, saying, I am innocent of the blood of this just person: see ye to it" (v. 24). But what Pilate calls being guilty would have corrupted the sacrifice, because he, being a Roman, was not fit to offer up a sacrifice to God. "Then answered all the people, and said, His blood be on us, and on our children" (v. 25). If there was any question as to where the weight of responsibility lay, it was crystal clear at that moment.

However, we may not be aware that in this entire process one high priest is making a judgment about another high priest. One high priest, Caiaphas, is from the Aaronic priesthood, the Old Testament order. The other high priest, Jesus, is of the order of Melchizedek, the new order. In the book of Hebrews, Jesus is repeatedly called "a priest for ever after the order of Melchisedec" (Hebrews 5:6; Psalm 110:4). Caiaphas is an earthly high priest; Jesus is a heavenly high priest. Caiaphas is justified in offering up a sacrifice on earth, because he serves in a temple made with hands. Jesus is a high priest after the order of Melchizedek, and He knows that sin will not be perfectly remitted until it goes beyond the mercy seat in the earth realm and goes to the mercy seat in the heavenly realm.

Read Hebrews 9:11–14 and get a sense of how profound Jesus as your high priest is to you.

The Transition from the Old to the New Order

What we are observing is the transition between orders: the former is giving way to the latter. The former is coming to an end, and its final act of atonement is to offer up Jesus to be the Savior of the world. To impart to you an understanding of this, I need to back up a bit.

The Old Testament tabernacle and temple on earth were shadows of which there is a heavenly temple in glory. God told Moses to make the tabernacle according to an exact pattern. When Moses got ready to build the tabernacle, and later when King Solomon built the temple, they were building according to God's pattern. My point is that while there was a pattern in the earth realm, it was patterned from what was in heaven. This is why God designed the temple Himself and gave explicit instructions, because He knew the pattern.

So now we have this contaminated, weak, carnal priest named Caiaphas, but he was necessary because the law requires that if there was to be a sacrifice, the priest has to offer it up. So the high priest offers up Jesus, thinking he was doing something for the people, but it was bigger than what he thinks it was. This was much more than just a political move; this was a move that would legally usher in salvation so that two thousand years later, "Whosoever shall call on the name of the Lord shall be saved" (Acts 2:21)!

Christ came before the high priest bound. He came before the priest bound because He was a sacrifice. Christ was bound to the Cross as the lamb was bound to the Old Testament altar. He was about to be offered up. "And I, if I be lifted up from the earth, will draw all men unto me" (John 12:32). So the priest gave his consent to the crucifixion, which changed what would merely be an execution into an offering unto God. Yet even while Jesus was dying as the Lamb of God with nails in His hands and feet, He was saving souls and setting people free. To one of the dying thieves on another cross, He said, "Verily I say unto thee, Today shalt thou be with me in paradise" (Luke 23:43).

One priesthood was giving way to a far superior priesthood. Caiaphas was the high priest over the old order. Jesus is the high priest over the new order which we are ushered into as a part of the priesthood: "Ye are a chosen generation, a royal priesthood, an holy nation, a peculiar people" (1 Peter 2:9). We can't be a royal priesthood if we don't have a high priest! When we understand the application of the blood of

Jesus as our high priest, it will wash off every curse, every spell, every depression, every generational curse, every suicide spirit, every demon that plagues us. The one thing that the devil doesn't want in a priest is the power of the blood, for the blood will set us free!

> *The application of the blood of Jesus as our high priest will wash off every curse, every spell, every depression, every generational curse, every suicide spirit, every demon that plagues us.*

There was also a debate during Jesus' trial where Pilate asked Jesus, "Art thou the King of the Jews?" and Jesus responded, "My kingdom is not of this world" (John 18:33, 36). In response to this exchange, "Pilate wrote a title, and put it on the cross. And the writing was JESUS OF NAZARETH THE KING OF THE JEWS. This title then read many of the Jews: for the place where Jesus was crucified was nigh to the city: and it was written in Hebrew, and Greek, and Latin. Then said the chief priests of the Jews to Pilate, Write not, The King of the Jews; but that he said, I am King of the Jews. Pilate answered, What I have written I have written" (John 19:19–22).

What we are seeing is the three-dimensional Christ as

our Prophet, Priest, and King. For the moment, we are seeing Christ as our High Priest, and we'll see Him as the King
later. Pilate's crown is a shadow of another crown that will
come when the twenty-four elders in the book of Revelation
cast their crowns at his feet (Revelation 4:10).

Jesus, Our High Priest in the Heavenlies

We have this old order coming to an end, and the high
priest was offering up Christ as a lamb. On the earth, Jesus
functioned as a lamb. But He was stepping into His priestly
office because though the blood of bullocks and goats had
covered sin on earth, it had not reached heaven. Christ's mis-
sion was to bring the blood to the mercy seat in heaven so that
we could "come boldly unto the throne of grace, that we may
obtain mercy, and find grace to help in time of need" (Hebrews 4:16). So when they hung Him high and they stretched
Him wide, they hung Him as a lamb, the Lamb of God. He
hung His head in the locks of His shoulders and said, "It is
finished" (John 19:3). What is finished? Every curse, every
spell, every bondage, and everything that is contrary to His
grace is finished!

Then they put the Lamb in a borrowed grave for three
days and three nights. But early Sunday morning, He rose

from the dead, got up out of the grave, and said, "Behold my hands and my feet, that it is I myself: handle me, and see; for a spirit hath not flesh and bones, as ye see me have" (Luke 24:39). The apostle Paul reflected on that sight and said, "O death, where

> *They put the Lamb in a borrowed grave for three days and three nights. But early Sunday morning, He rose from the dead.*

is thy sting? O grave, where is thy victory?" (1 Corinthians 15:55). Jesus rose up with all power in His hand, and He could rightfully say, "All power is given unto me in heaven and in earth" (Matthew 28:18). Paul adds: "Wherefore God also hath highly exalted him, and given him a name which is above every name: That at the name of Jesus every knee should bow, of things in heaven, and things in earth, and things under the earth; and that every tongue should confess that Jesus Christ is Lord, to the glory of God the Father" (Philippians 2:9–11).

Christ rose from the grave and approached Mary Magdalene in the garden. When she finally recognized that He was the risen Christ, she reached out to touch Him, but He said, "Touch me not; for I am not yet ascended to my Father: but go to my brethren, and say unto them, I ascend unto my

Father, and your Father; and to my God, and your God" (John 20:17). He said that because He was moving into His role as the High Priest. First, Jesus must ascend to heaven with the blood, and He doesn't want her to contaminate Him. His purpose is to take the blood beyond the heavenly veil.

Understand that there were three veils. I have already mentioned the veil in the temple between the Holy Place and the Holy of Holies. When Christ died, this veil was rent from the top to the bottom. Never say it was ripped from the bottom to the top, because it could then be said the old order ripped it. It was ripped from the top to the bottom, which means the new order has ripped open the old order.

The second veil is the veil of His flesh. When the Roman soldier pierced Jesus' side, He opened up the veil of His flesh so that we could be in Christ. The ripping of His flesh is symbolic of going from the physical body of Christ to the mystical body of Christ. "Having therefore, brethren, boldness to enter into the holiest by the blood of Jesus, by a new and living way, which he hath consecrated for us, through the veil, that is to say, his flesh" (Hebrews 10:19–20). It wasn't just so the blood could get out; it was also so that you and I could get in. This is why the apostle Paul repeatedly takes our position from being "with Christ" in the Gospels to being "in Christ" in his epistles: "There is therefore now no condemnation to them who are *in Christ Jesus*. . . . If any man be *in Christ*, he is a new creation. . . . You are accepted *in the Beloved*. . . . *In Him* I live . . . *in Him* I move . . . *in Him* I have my being."

The third veil is the veil in the heavenlies, where only the High Priest could go as the first fruits of the resurrection. So when Christ was raised from the dead, Matthew says that "many holy people who had died were raised to life" and seen walking the streets of Jerusalem (Matthew 27:52–53). The reason they were walking the streets of Jerusalem is that they could not pierce the heavenly veil. Christ had to be the first fruits of the resurrection, so they had to wait down here until He pierced the third veil. Acts 1:9–11 states that Jesus ascended on high before His disciples, then an angel said, "Ye men of Galilee, why stand ye gazing up into heaven? this same Jesus, which is taken up from you into heaven, shall so come in like manner as ye have seen him go into heaven." Jesus went in first, and "when he ascended up on high, he led captivity captive" (Ephesians 4:8).

The Holy of Holies

I want you to understand the Holy of Holies, because that is what is beyond the veil. There is only one piece of furniture in the Holy of Holies—the Ark of the Covenant, which is a picture of Christ. It is made out of wood, a perishable substance, to represent the humanity of Christ. It is laid over in gold, to represent the divinity of Christ. It was also inlaid with gold, so we must realize that it was not just that God was in Christ, but also that Christ was in God.

In the Ark of the Covenant, there are three items: "wherein was the golden pot that had manna, and Aaron's rod that budded, and the tables of the covenant" (Hebrews 9:4). First, there was Aaron's rod—an old stick that was dry and dead and budded and blossomed and brought forth fruit. This promises resurrection life after death. This assures us that death is swallowed up in life.

Second, there was a pot of manna. This promises us that God's provision toward us is so perfect and so eternal that this is the one pot of manna that didn't go bad the next day. It also tells us that Jesus is our sufficiency, that He is our bread of life, and that if we eat His flesh and drink His blood, we can live in heaven with Him forever.

Third, the Ark also had the first set of the Ten Commandment tablets that were broken, for we had broken the law before we ever got it. When Moses comes down from Mount Sinai with the tablets, he found the people of Israel had broken the commandments before they ever received them. God wants

> *Through the law, He has asked us for a righteousness He knows we cannot do; He has asked us for a holiness that He knows we cannot produce.*

us to know that through the law shall no flesh be justified. Through the law, He has asked us for a righteousness that He knows we cannot do; He has asked us for a holiness that He knows we cannot produce. And if you tell me that you are righteous on your own, I will tell you it's a lie, because "there is none that doeth good, no, not one" (Romans 3:12).

The Ark of the Covenant had long sticks on either side so that it could be carried, letting us know that our God is mobile. He's not a monument; He's a movement. He's progressive. He's flowing. Our God is alive and always moving (see Genesis 1:2). That is why religion frustrates us, because religion is stagnant, but walking with God is a moving thing, a growing thing, a developing thing.

The top of the Ark of the Covenant has the mercy seat. This is the place where God looks down and decides judgment based on the law that we can't keep. The law is against us, and the only way that God doesn't judge us for sin is "when I see the blood, I will pass over you" (Exodus 12:13). Under the old order of the Old Testament, since they didn't have an efficacious blood, they used temporary blood—the blood of bullocks and goats, which covered the law for a year. But Jesus, when He went through the heavenly veil, put the efficacious and eternal blood of God on the real mercy seat, of which the one on earth was just a shadow. He put the blood on the mercy seat so that God cannot see the law when He looks at us. We are secure under the eternal blood of Jesus.

Regarding the blood, when the priest in the old order got ready to come into the Holy of Holies, he came in with a sacrifice to be offered up, if not the whole lamb then the sprinkling of the blood. So the priest of the old-order went in with another object, offering atonement for his own sins and for the people (see Leviticus 23). But in the new order, Jesus is sinless: so as our High Priest, He didn't need to offer up a sacrifice for His own sin. Jesus is both the High Priest and the sacrifice, the Lamb. "But Christ being come an high priest of good things to come, by a greater and more perfect tabernacle, not made with hands, that is to say, not of this building; neither by the blood of goats and calves, but by his own blood he entered in once into the holy place, having obtained eternal redemption for us (Hebrews 9:11–12).

A Living Sacrifice

We see this language of the priesthood in Romans 12:1: "I beseech you therefore, brethren, by the mercies of God, that ye present your bodies a living sacrifice, holy, acceptable unto God, which is your reasonable service." Paul begs and pleads with us, as members of the family of God, for that is who we are under His mercy. At one time, we were "aliens from the commonwealth of Israel, and strangers from the covenants of promise" (Ephesians 2:12), but through Christ we have been adopted into the royal family and have "received the Spirit of adoption, whereby we cry, Abba, Father" (Romans 8:15). Now we are sons and daughters of God, and we are joint heirs with Jesus Christ. Because He has opened up the heavenly veil, we can come boldly into the throne of grace, and our first priestly act is to offer ourselves to God as a living sacrifice.

So how do we do that? We don't have an altar on which to be tied. How does God offer us up? Through the things in our lives that we are tied to, that hurt us, and that break our will. It might be that a difficult marriage is the place of our sacrifice. Or the job that is driving us crazy. We asked God to change something in our lives, but He didn't remove it because He is using it as the place of a living sacrifice. It might be the relationship with a child that won't get better and won't change, that has humbled us and brought us to our knees, that has made us weep and cry, that has made us pray and seek God. God says, "I want you to understand what I am trying to raise you. This is the place of your sacrifice."

> *Every one of us has something in our lives we are tied to that breaks our heart.*

Every one of us has something in our lives we are tied to that breaks our heart. God uses that place in our lives so we can legitimately be a priest unto God and say, "Though he slay me, yet will I trust in him" (Job 13:15). There is something that God left in our lives amidst all of His other blessings, that one thing that doesn't work in our lives—the priesthood is the place of our sacrifice, where we smile through our tears. Every believer is living his or her life in one area or another as a living sacrifice.

It is a sacrifice, but I have to do it! It's a living sacrifice, but I've got to give it! It's a sacrifice, but I have to be it! It's a sacrifice that is holy and acceptable to God!

Close your eyes for a minute and find your living altar.

What hurts your flesh?
What works on your will?
What gets on your nerves?
What never happened for you like it happened for other people?

Perhaps you have never been more spiritually alive in your life, but when it comes to that "thing," you are tied up. You may have rebuked the devil and stood against the enemy, but you are still tied—it's because it is not a devil that has you tied. God has given you something to keep you on our knees, to keep you humble. And if you can be tied and still worship, if you can be lonely and still worship, if you can go through tests and trials and embarrassment and pain and still worship, if you can lift your hands and say hallelu-jah, if you can say yes to God with tears running down your face, then you are beginning to be just a little bit like Jesus, who said, "Nevertheless not my will, but thine, be done" (Luke 22:42).

Can you worship God
through testing and pain and trials?

If you can still lift up your hands
through all your wounds and all your pain
and all your bruising and still praise the Lord,
it will go up to God as a sweet-smelling savor!

The Father is seeking those to worship Him
in spirit and in truth!

Whatever your situation.
if you praise God,
you will be a living sacrifice!

Lift your hands!
Open your mouth, royal priesthood!
Come wounded, come bruised,
come trapped, come tired,
come tied, come lonely.

Royal priesthood!
Give Him the glory!

THE PRESENCE OF THE SPIRIT ENDUES
MEN WITH DIVINE AUTHORITY AND
POWER. THE HOLY GHOST DOES
NOT COME UPON METHODS, BUT
UPON MEN. HE DOES NOT ANOINT
MACHINERY, BUT MEN. HE DOES NOT
WORK THROUGH ORGANIZATIONS,
BUT THROUGH MEN. HE DOES NOT
DWELL IN BUILDINGS, BUT IN MEN.

—*Samuel Chadwick*

Chapter 6

THE MASTER'S MYSTERIOUS PLAN

I recently spoke at Southeastern University in Florida, and I was telling the students that one of the signs of a great leader is that he or she is given to great detail. Of course, God is the ultimate leader, and He is given to the most intricate of details for the care and nurture of our lives. Our God is that awesome! He who has a strategy for the universe also has a plan for our lives, and His plan is awesome!

One of the things we need to understand about God is not just that He is awesome, although He is; not just that He is good, although He is; not just that He is righteous, although He is; not just that He is holy and perfect and pure, although He is. God is also intelligent and wise. If we do not understand that He is intelligent, and we see Him only as powerful, then we should be fearful, because power in the wrong hands is a dangerous thing. The only way we are confident about power is when we know that the one who holds the power is regulated by wisdom and intelligence. God is intelligent; He is infinitely intellectual; He is infinitely wise. Thus we trust Him with His great power.

God is a strategist. He has a master plan that He laid out before the foundation of the world. Isn't it amazing to know that we are in the plan of God? He is so given to detail that He included you and me in the specifications of what He has ordained and predestined to occur. Catch the wonderment in the words of the psalmist David: "What is man, that thou art mindful of him? And the son of man, that thou visitest him?" (Psalm 8:4). It is mind-boggling to consider that a God who runs galaxies and hemispheres and stratospheres would be so engaged that "the very hairs of your head are all numbered" (Matthew 10:30). That is what I call attention to detail.

God's Master Plan Set in Motion

The apostle Paul begins to deal with the master plan of God in 1 Corinthians 2:1–11.

And I, brethren, when I came to you, came not with excellency of speech or of wisdom, declaring unto you the testimony of God. For I determined not to know any thing among you, save Jesus Christ, and him crucified. And I was with you in weakness, and in fear, and in much trembling. And my speech and my preaching was not with enticing words of man's wisdom, but in demonstration of the Spirit and of power: That your faith should not stand in the wisdom of men, but in the power of God.

Howbeit we speak wisdom among them that are perfect: yet not the wisdom of this world, nor of the princes of this world, that come to nought: But we speak the wisdom of God in a mystery, even the hidden wisdom, which God ordained before the world unto our glory: Which none of the princes of this world knew: for had they known it, they would not have crucified the Lord of glory.

But as it is written, Eye hath not seen, nor ear heard, neither have entered into the heart of man, the things which God hath prepared for them that love him.

But God hath revealed them unto us by his Spirit: for the Spirit searcheth all things, yea, the deep things of God. For what man knoweth the things of a man, save the spirit of man which is in him? Even so the things of God knoweth no man, but the Spirit of God.

Paul said he didn't try to impress the Corinthians with his articulation or his oratorical abilities. He did not speak in the language of the intellectual, that is, "the wisdom of this world"; nor was he the boy of the politicians, that is, "of the princes of this world." Paul was not controlled by the Roman government or by the aristocracy or by the religious in-stitutions or by the intellectual regimes. "But," Paul says, "we speak the wisdom of God in a mystery, even the hidden wis-dom, which God ordained before the world unto our glory."

I refer to this as "the Master's Mysterious Plan Set in Mo-tion."

So, how do we relegate in our own thinking the plan or, as Paul calls it, the purpose of God, the master strategy of God against the plans of the enemy? We have studied the plot of the high priest Caiaphas that began the demise of Christ. So let's use Jesus as a template to begin to better understand what happened in His life, but also what happens in our lives.

Consider the pressure Jesus was constantly under. He had a group of disciples who did not understand His mis-sion. Some of them were wor-ried about who would get to sit on His right hand and on His left in glory. Some wanted Him to overthrow the political power of Rome so that the Jews would be emancipated and be able to possess their land again with-out any outside interference. He had one guy on his board of trustees who was stealing money and setting up a plot to

> *Consider the pressure Jesus was constantly under.*

sell Jesus for thirty pieces of silver. As sanctioned by the high priest, the most religious people of His day—the scribes, Sadducees, and Pharisees—were setting an entrapment to kill Him. He was the most controversial, most spiritual leader of His era. He was on the hit list from hell, and all the while He was turning water into wine, healing the sick, raising the dead, and blessing prostitutes. We would break apart at the seams under such stress.

Bad news is, God didn't stop the plots that were set against Christ, but He used their plots to bring Christ into His purpose and destiny. For instance, at the Last Supper with His disciples, I believe that is why Jesus said to Judas, "That thou doest, do quickly" (John 13:27). He knew that although Judas had purposed to join the plot to destroy Him, he was being used by God to push Him into His destiny.

When Paul talks about the wisdom of God, it is so awesome that it includes the plots of our enemies. That means God included the hatred of our enemies toward us in His plan. Rather than God warring against our enemies' plots and plans, He uses them to push us closer into our destinies, so we can say, "It was good for us that they hated us, because their hatred helped us get into a place where God wanted us to be."

If you need proof of this truth, I submit for further evidence that Joseph's brothers played into God's plan when they threw Joseph into the pit and then sold him into slavery. Joseph's destiny could not be fulfilled in his home country, and as horribly as they treated Joseph, it was within God's purpose. Joseph had to be in Egypt at a particular time to bless his brethren; and their hatred was the wings that God used to bring him into the place God wanted him to be. Later, after Joseph had fulfilled his destiny, he could say to his brothers, "But as for you, ye thought evil against me; but God meant it unto good, to bring to pass, as it is this day, to save much people alive" (Genesis 50:20).

What I'm trying to get you to see is that even in the crucifixion of Christ, "All things work together for good to them that love God, to them who are the called according to his purpose" (Romans 8:28). The "all things" are not just about the John the Baptists and the Peters who loved Him; it was also about the Judas-incidence that worked good for Jesus. We need a Judas in our lives. We need a high priest who is sabotaging our lives, because God has included it in the quilt of our destinies. God, as the Master Planner, is careful to implement what our enemies mean for evil and make it for good. If you have been called according to the purposes of the Master's mysterious plan, it's all working for your good.

As difficult as it is at the time, it might mean being left with two children, or a husband who won't pay child support, or both. It might mean having your wife walk away from your marriage for another man or because you put your faith in Christ. It might mean never knowing your birth mother or father. Sometimes it takes until we are thirty or forty before we look back and say, "Lord, I thank You that I grew up as I did, in the place that I did, in the circumstances that I did, with the people that I did! I thank You because it shaped me, it molded me, it helped me, it matured me, it established me! It taught me how to pray and trust in You. You taught me how to stand on my own. I am stronger and wiser and tougher through Christ. Thank You!" Stop wishing you were someone else and thank the Lord that He has a master strategy that is shaping your life.

It is of this strategy that the apostle Paul writes when he says that if the princes of this world had understood the master plan, they would never have crucified the Lord. They were pawns in the hand of the Master, who used their malice and the malady of their melodrama to execute the divine purpose of God, and they never even knew it! They didn't know that

Jesus was the Lamb; they thought He was a heretic. They didn't know He was the High Priest; they thought He was a con man. Some of His enemies thought they were doing God a service by killing Him. They executed their plots against Jesus because they didn't know who He was, and in doing so they set in motion some things that were unstoppable for God's purpose.

The same is true in our lives. Some people seem determined to make our lives difficult, yet God uses their attitude to showcase us, to position us. He uses someone's criticism to keep us uncomfortable, so we won't settle into mediocrity. He uses their malice to bring out our best, because sometimes it is a fact that other people's hate makes us stronger and better and more perfected in what we do.

> *Some people seem determined to make our lives difficult, yet God uses their attitude to showcase us, to position us.*

God has a strategy, a plan that supersedes all the plots of those who come against us. He considered their plots when He made the plan, and He made their plots serve His plan. While they don't know God's plan for us, they also don't know that God's knows about their plots against us; and He

174

is working it all together to maneuver us to the place we need to be for the good of His own divine purpose.

Passover Leads to Pentecost

My intent is to help you bridge over from the Passion of Passover to Pentecost, and to do that I need to provide a deeper understanding of both events. Passover is Old Testament terminology that points us to the Cross in the New Testament. The celebration of Pentecost in the Old Testament is translated in the New Testament as the powerful occurrence of the outpouring of the Holy Spirit upon the disciples when they were gathered in the upper room spoken of in Acts 2. Many people think that Pentecost started in the book of Acts, but they fail to see it in the full context of its Old Testament origin.

To provide the background for Pentecost requires first understanding the Feast of the Passover. The Feast of the Passover is a celebration that is still celebrated today among those who are Orthodox and traditional Jews. It commemorates the night when Moses led the children of Israel out of Egypt. I recommend that you read Exodus 12 to gather the whole experience in your mind. On the day of Passover in Egypt, all the children of Israel who were in covenant with God were required to sacrifice a lamb and place blood on the doorpost and on the lintel of their dwellings. God said, "When I see the blood, I will pass over you" (v. 13), but at every home that did not have blood on it, the death angel stopped, went in, and took a life. Hence we have the annual Feast of the Passover, because the children of Israel knew they had been spared only through and by the auspicious grace of the blood of the lamb.

What you may not know is why the death angel passed over. The death angel did not pass over as an act of God's mercy or because the people in the house were forgiven. The death angel passed over because when he saw the blood, it was a sign that death had already visited that house! There was no need to go and revisit that house with death, because death was already there. What mattered was the blood. It wasn't the individual who died; it was the lamb that died for the house so that the people in the house could live. Thus the children of Israel came out of the land of Egypt by the blood of the lamb.

After Hurricane Katrina, I went to New Orleans to be part of the team that began to bless and challenge the workers who were searching homes for dead bodies. Once a search had been done on a house, they would put a mark on the outside of the house so no one else would waste time going through the house again. That principle goes all the way back to the book of Exodus. When the Israelites put the blood on the doorpost and lintel, it was a sign that there was no need to come into that house; death had already hit that house. Through the death of our Lamb of God, we are free and whole, and as long as we stay under the blood, "No weapon that is formed against thee shall prosper" (Isaiah 54:17).

In essence, that is what launched the Feast of the Passover, but we need to go even deeper. When Moses came to the burning bush in the wilderness and had his marvelous encounter with God, God said to Moses, "I will send thee unto Pharaoh, that thou mayest bring forth my people the children of Israel out of Egypt" (Exodus 3:10). God wanted His people to be liberated, but not just so they could be free and not just so they could go to the Promised Land. God's purpose was that His people "may sacrifice to the LORD our God" (v. 18). Moses' assignment was to go down to Egypt and lead the people back to where he and they could worship God. The emancipation that provoked the liberation of the children of Israel was not so they could buy big houses in the Promised Land and eat fat grapes; it was so that they could have a face-to-face with their God and be reconnected to Him in the wilderness.

The Feast of the Passover celebrates the Israelites' liberation, which was followed by the Feast of Pentecost. When the children of Israel were liberated from their Egyptian oppressor, fifty days later they found themselves at Mt. Sinai, where the glory of the Lord encompassed the mountain and the entire mountain was on fire because of His glory (Exodus 19). Here they had an encounter with God that was celebrated as the Feast of Pentecost, or the Feast of the Harvest, because Pentecost sets its watch from the Passover. If Passover is the seed, Pentecost is the harvest.

Here is how the Feast of Pentecost was declared in Leviticus 23:15–22 following the Passover celebration:

And ye shall count unto you from the morrow after the sabbath, from the day that ye brought the sheaf of the wave offering; seven sabbaths shall be complete: Even unto the morrow after the seventh sabbath shall ye number fifty days; and ye shall offer a new meat offering unto the LORD. Ye shall bring out of your habitations two wave loaves of two tenth deals; they shall be of fine flour; they shall be baken with leaven; they are the firstfruits unto the LORD. And ye shall offer with the bread seven lambs without blemish of the first year, and one young bullock, and two rams: they shall be for a burnt offering unto the LORD, with their meat offering, and their drink offerings, even an offering made by fire, of sweet savour unto the LORD. Then ye shall sacrifice one kid of the goats for a sin offering, and two lambs of the first year for a sacrifice of peace offerings. And the priest shall wave them with the bread of the firstfruits for a wave offering before the LORD, *with the two lambs: they shall be holy to the* LORD *for the priest. And ye shall proclaim on the selfsame day, that it may be an holy convocation unto you: ye shall do no servile work therein: it shall be a statute for ever in all your dwellings throughout your generations.*

And when ye reap the harvest of your land, thou shalt not make clean riddance of the corners of thy field when thou reapest, neither shalt thou gather any gleaning of thy harvest: thou shalt leave them unto the poor, and to the stranger: I am the LORD *your God.*

Why do they call it Pentecost? The Greeks, actually, began calling it Pentecost. *Pentecost* means "fiftieth day" and is celebrated fifty days after the Passover.

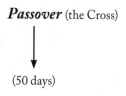

Passover (the Cross)

(50 days)

Pentecost (outpouring of the Holy Spirit)

Passover came so that they could have the Pentecost. It is possible to have Passover without Pentecost, but it is impossible to have Pentecost without Passover. In other words, it is

> *It is possible to have Passover without Pentecost, but it is impossible to have Pentecost without Passover.*

possible to experience the Cross and not Pentecost, but it is impossible to experience Pentecost if you have not been through the Cross.

We are talking about order: first comes this, then comes that. Pentecost happens fifty days after the Passover. If you don't kill the Lamb, there will be no Pentecost. But if you slay the Lamb, you set in motion Pentecost. When they crucified Jesus, they set some things in motion that were unstoppable. Pentecost was going to happen, and they couldn't stop it, they couldn't kill it. They crucified Jesus to stop Him from doing His works on the earth; but when they crucified Him, greater works began to break out among His people. After Pentecost, instead of God working through just one Man, He began to work through every believer. They set in motion something so unstoppable that two thousand years later it is still marching forward and cannot be stopped.

Pentecost sets its watch by the Passover. Fifty days after Passover happened, the power of God was released. Fifty days after Passover comes Pentecost in the Old Testament, and it is an illustration on which the New Testament is predicated.

The Blood upon the Mercy Seat

Had they never crucified the Lord, all they would have had to contend with was the blood of bullocks and goats being reapplied to the mercy seat on earth every year. But when Jesus took His blood and went through the heavenlies into the Holy of Holies, it started something so powerful that it was unstoppable! This has everything to do with why we are free in Christ today.

> We are not free because we sing worship songs.
> We are not free because we stopped smoking.
> We are not free because we go to the Father's house faithfully.
> We are not free because we carry a Bible around that we never read.
> We are not free because we wear a cross around our neck or because we have the sign of the fish on our car or because we possess all the symbols of salvation.
> We have to understand what provokes our liberation!

The Old Testament is the schoolmaster that teaches us the grace of the New Testament. The Old Testament is in shadow what the New Testament is in reality. If something is true in the Old Testament, it is true in the New. There is a continuity of truth—it either is truth or it isn't. In the Old Testament, God teaches us what the high priest will do every year on the Day of Atonement. This was the Holy Spirit giving us instructions on what Jesus would do to bring about our deliverance. It was a dress rehearsal in the Old Testament that was set in motion in the New Testament by the crucifixion of Jesus. Every year the high priests redid the atonement sacrifice—it was a dress rehearsal.

We studied the tabernacle with the twelve tribes of Israel all gathered around it. They were watching on the Day of Atonement, because they had prayed and asked forgiveness of their sins. They were ready for the high priest to go into the Holy of Holies, the place where the fire falls, the Shekinah glory. This was where the Spirit of God fell on the mercy seat, where sin was eradicated, where judgment was allocated, where freedom was instituted, and where liberation was consecrated. It was there in the Holy of Holies that one Day of Atonement for sins determined what the next 364 days would be like.

All the people's tents around the tabernacle were facing the place where the high priest was to go in, because they

The Master's Mysterious Plan

were watching and waiting to hear that the blood had hit the mercy seat, for if the blood did not hit the mercy seat, they had no peace with God. But if the high priest, who was the only one allowed inside the Holy of Holies, made it into the Holy of Holies with the blood, and if the blood hit the mercy seat and the priest lived, it meant that all their sins, no matter how grotesque, were forgiven and eradicated by the blood of the lamb.

What they practiced in the Old Testament is a picture of what Jesus did for us, only this time He was not going into a tent or through a veil that was created by the hands of men. Jesus was carrying His own blood into the temple not made with hands, behind the veil into the Holy of Holies, to offer up redemption for our sin. He was going beyond where any human eye can see, and He was going behind the veil to put the blood on the heavenly mercy seat of which the Old Testament mercy seat was only a shadow. He places His blood upon the mercy seat so that our salvation is ratified. Thus we can and should sing, "My hope is built on nothing less than Jesus' blood and righteousness."

The Sound of a Mighty Rushing Wind

The Old Testament also teaches us about the garments of the high priest. His garments reflected the garments on the door of the tabernacle: blue for God's grace, red for His redemption, white for His holiness. The "robe" of the ephod, all of blue, worn immediately under the ephod, was without seam or sleeves, and the hem or skirt was ornamented with golden bells and pomegranates, seventy-two of each in alternate order. The bottom of the high priest's garment represented redemption. When the priest got ready to go into the Holy of Holies, he entered the tabernacle or temple before all the people adorned in his immaculate priestly vestments, then laid them aside and assumed only his servant's attire of a sacred linen tunic as well as the linen sash and linen turban and with linen undergarments next to his skin. The people couldn't see him when he went behind the veil to put the blood on the mercy seat, but they could listen for him. The sounding of the bells intimated to the priests in

> As he began to put his garments back on, "the sound" was a sign that the blood had hit the mercy seat and the high priest was alive.

the outer court the time when the high priest entered into the Holy of Holies. As he began to put his garments back on, "the sound" was a sign that the blood had hit the mercy seat and the high priest was alive; it was a sign that they had another year of peace with God, a reinstated relationship of At-one-ment with God.

Just so, just before Jesus ascended into heaven and went behind the true (being the third) veil as our High Priest, He instructed His disciples "that they should not depart from Jerusalem, but wait for the promise of the Father, which, saith he, ye have heard of me. For John truly baptized with water; but ye shall be baptized with the Holy Ghost not many days hence" (Acts 1:4–5). And when the day of Pentecost was fully come and they were in one place in one accord, suddenly there came a sound; but instead of the sound of bells, it was a mighty rushing wind! This sound was a sign that our High Priest was not dead, but that He ever lives to make intercession for us that whosoever shall call on the name of the Lord shall be saved. The sound is the sign! If the high priest went into the Holy of Holies and the blood was not received, the high priest would die and all peace with God would be destroyed. But if he was alive, they could hear the bells ringing; and the bells ringing was a sign that he lived.

Thus, Jesus told His disciples, Don't start preaching until you hear the sound. But when you hear the sound, "ye shall be witnesses unto me both in Jerusalem, and in all Judaea, and in Samaria, and unto the uttermost part of the earth" (Acts 1:8). And when the day of Pentecost came fifty days after the Cross, there was a sound! Can you imagine what it was like to be in the upper room and hear such a sound as that? Acts 2:1–4 states,

> *And when the day of Pentecost was fully come, they were all with one accord in one place. And suddenly there came a sound from heaven as of a rushing mighty wind, and it filled all the house where they were sitting. And there appeared unto them cloven tongues like as of fire, and it sat upon each of them. And they were all filled with the Holy Ghost, and began to speak with other tongues, as the Spirit gave them utterance.*

At that same time, God-fearing Jews from every nation under heaven were staying in Jerusalem. They had come to Jerusalem to celebrate the Feast of Pentecost, or the Feast of the Harvest, and they were bringing their harvest to do business. Hearing this sound, they gathered together and were bewildered because they heard their own languages being spoken from this upper room. And they were amazed because they understood that the speakers were from Galilee. Jews from all over the world heard the wonders of God being declared in their own language, and they rightly asked, "What does this mean?" Some people made fun of it and said they were just drunk.

Peter, however, came out and spoke to the people, declaring that the men were not drunk. No, he said, "This is that which was spoken by the prophet Joel; and it shall come to pass in the last days, saith God, I will pour out of my Spirit upon all flesh: and your sons and your daughters shall prophesy, and your young men shall see visions, and your old men shall dream dreams: and on my servants and on my handmaidens I will pour out in those days of my Spirit; and they shall prophesy" (Acts 2:16–18). This is the harvest toward which the Passover and the Cross pointed. God wants to *pour* the Holy Spirit out!

Remember, the sound was merely a sign. It was a sign that the blood of Jesus had been applied to the mercy seat, but the sound was not a sign of the indwelling of the Holy Spirit. If it were, every time in the Bible that someone was filled with the Holy Spirit, there would be the sound of a mighty rushing wind, the house would shake, and cloven tongues of fire would set upon their heads. That only happened one time.

In Acts 10, when the Roman centurion Cornelius and his kinsmen and friends received the baptism of the Holy Ghost, there was no sound from heaven, no mighty rushing wind, no cloven tongues of fire. It simply says that the Holy Spirit "fell" upon them, and "they heard them speak with tongues, and magnify God" (v. 46). In Acts 19:1–6, another group of disciples received the baptism of the Holy Spirit, but the only sound they heard was their speaking in tongues and prophesying (see v. 6). These disciples had believed in Jesus and repented, but they had not even heard of, let alone received, the Holy Spirit. The speaking in tongues was a sign that they were filled with the Holy Spirit, not that they were saved. You can be saved and not speak in tongues. If you are filled to overflowing with the Holy Ghost, there will be evidence. Much like you fill a cup with liquid to the point it can't hold any more and it spills over the side, that is the outward sign of an inward filling.

Why did the day of Pentecost, with the regalia that surrounded it as described in Acts 2, only happen once?

When the Day of Pentecost Was Fully Come

Note the words of Acts 2:1, for they are important: *And when the day of Pentecost was fully come.* Having followed what

I've taught through this entire book, I hope you can now see that this had been coming for thousands of years—in every shadow and in every type of the Old Testament, it was coming. From the promise of redemption in Genesis 3:15, all of it was pointing toward this day of a full restoration of relationship with God. Jesus taught His disciples lesson after lesson about the coming and the role of the Holy Spirit after His death and resurrection. For forty days after His resurrection, "he shewed himself alive after his passion by many infallible proofs" (Acts 1:3). He left on the fortieth day, which means they waited ten days by themselves, after His departure, for the coming of the Spirit.

Then "suddenly there came a sound from heaven," and we join all those who were gathered there to watch *the inaugural service of the Holy Spirit*. There is the wind and the shaking and cloven tongues of fire—that's a parade of signs! "And they were all filled with the Holy Ghost, and began to speak with other tongues, as the Spirit gave them utterance."

I hope you noticed that the Holy Spirit *sat* upon the believers. This means that now the Holy Spirit has moved into His

> *I hope you noticed that the Holy Spirit* sat *upon the believers.*

judicious position of authority in the earth realm, and that He rules and reigns with us. This is the regalia of God's eternal Kingdom being established on earth! This is why we only see it one time! This was the inaugural service of the Holy Spirit's influence over our dispensation!

Remember that Pentecost ties back to the experience of the children of Israel at Mount Sinai that burned with fire, which was also an inaugural service. For the children of Israel left Egypt as slaves, crossed through the Red Sea, and became sons; but they did not become a nation until they got to the mountain and entered into a relationship with God by faith. So from the inaugural service at Mount Sinai to the inaugural service at Pentecost, the one consecrates a kingdom and the other consecrates a King as the Holy Spirit sets up His rule and reign—thus the regalia!

We see in this a change in the relationship of God and mankind. Throughout the books of Matthew, Mark, Luke, and John, Jesus was "Emmanuel," the dwells-among-us God. However, He taught His disciples this about the Holy Spirit in John 14:16–20:

> *I will pray the Father, and he shall give you another Comforter, that he may abide with you for ever; even the Spirit of truth; whom the world cannot receive, because it*

seeth him not, neither knoweth him; but ye know him; for he dwelleth with you, and shall be in you. I will not leave you comfortless: I will come to you. Yet a little while, and the world seeth me no more; but ye see me: because I live, ye shall live also. At that day ye shall know that I am in my Father, and ye in me, and I in you.

He no longer is the dwells-among-us God; He is the dwell-in-us God. Through this new relationship we have come into an intimacy that we have never had with God before.

The fact that the Holy Spirit now "dwelleth with you and shall be in you" is hugely significant. Up until Acts 2, He visited people. The Spirit came upon the prophet Ezekiel, came upon Moses, came upon Joshua, and came upon many other Old Testament believers to do a work. But now the Holy Spirit is not visiting anymore; now He is indwelling. He abides with us forever. Whether or not we, as believers, feel Him, He is with us. Whether or not we sense Him, He is there!

We should also be aware that the Holy Spirit is *the restrainer*. When the antichrist and the spirit of the antichrist comes to take over the world, it is the Holy Spirit who restrains him and holds him back. The Holy Spirit says, "You cannot touch what I have blessed!" "When the enemy shall come in like a flood, the Spirit of the LORD shall lift up a standard against him" (Isaiah 59:19). The reason the witch can't hex you, and the devil can't curse you, and your enemies can't destroy you is because the Holy Spirit is a restrainer that stops the enemy. In fact, the Holy Spirit continues to restrain the antichrist. According to 2 Thessalonians 2, the only thing stopping "the man of sin" from being revealed in his power is that the Holy Spirit restrains him from doing what he wants to do. To God be the glory!

Let us remind ourselves that if we are walking in victory and faith, it is not because of our own strength. As long as the Spirit of God is in the earth, even while we sleep, the Spirit of God is restraining the enemy. God is fighting for us in ways we can never even imagine. "Be not afraid nor dismayed by reason of this great multitude; for the battle is not yours, but God's. . . . Ye shall not need to fight in this battle: set yourselves, stand ye still, and see the salvation of the LORD with you" (2 Chronicles 20:15, 17). If you ever get that sense that something or someone was fighting for you, and you wonder how you made it through a certain circumstance, the Lord brought you through! The Holy Ghost has been fighting for you all your life! You should give God a praise offering!

The Holy Spirit is also *our Rabbi*, our Master Teacher.

Jesus said, "Howbeit when he, the Spirit of truth, is come, he will guide you into all truth: for he shall not speak of himself; but whatsoever he shall hear, that shall he speak: and he will shew you things to come" (John 16:13). In 1 Corinthians 2, which we studied at the beginning of this chapter, Paul, who spoke five different languages, declared that the hidden mysteries that he taught had not been learned in a school, but by sitting at the feet of our Rabbi. "But God hath revealed them unto us by his Spirit: for the Spirit searcheth all things, yea, the deep things of God. For what man knoweth the things of a man, save the spirit of man which is in him? Even so the things of God knoweth no man, but the Spirit of God."

The Holy Spirit and You

When the Holy Spirit sat down on the believers at Pentecost, He moved into power, and He poured His power into the believers that they might be His witnesses.

If you haven't been filled with the Holy Spirit, God will fill you! If you have been filled, but you haven't been letting Him reign, let Him reign! You must go from Passover to Pentecost! Stop fighting these battles with your flesh! This is too much for you! You need to loose the power of the Holy Spirit and let Him fight for you. God wants to give you rest, and He wants to work for you. As long as you continue to try to do God's work, He cannot work in your life until you rest. Then the Holy Spirit can constrain you to move into the life abundantly He has planned for you and restrains the enemy from destroying all that God has ordained for you. The Holy Spirit is fighting for you!

When the deacon Stephen was about to be stoned to death by the Sanhedrin for his fearless declaration of the death and resurrection of Jesus, we are told: "But he, being full of the Holy Ghost, looked up stedfastly into heaven, and saw the glory of God, and Jesus standing on the right hand of God, and said, Behold, I see the heavens opened, and the Son of man standing on the right hand of God" (Acts 7:55–56). Stephen didn't even care about his fate, because he saw beyond the heavenly veil and saw our living High Priest standing up and the Holy Spirit sitting down over this era. He looked up and began to glorify God. That's what we should do when people are trying to stone us—look up into heaven and glorify God.

Ask God for an outpouring of the Holy Spirit.

Ask God to restore, revive, refresh, and renew.

Ask God to rest on your life.

God wants to pour the Holy Spirit out!—

not drop it out,

not dribble it out,

not mist it out!

God wants to pour it out!

Pour it out on our lives!

Pour it out on our families!

Pour it out on our finances!

Pour it out on our bodies!

God wants to pour out His Spirit

until our sons and daughters

are drunk in the Holy Spirit!

THERE IS NOT A SINGLE BELIEVER WHO READS THIS PAGE WHO MAY NOT CLAIM A SHARE IN THE PENTECOSTAL GIFT. THE SPIRIT MAY BE IN US, REGENERATING AND RENEWING US, BUT IT IS NECESSARY THAT HE SHOULD BE ON US ALSO, AS HE DESCENDED AND REMAINED ON JESUS IN HIS BAPTISM, IF WE ARE TO FULFILL OUR MINISTRY TO MANKIND. WE ARE NOT RESTRICTED IN GOD, BUT OURSELVES. WE HAVE NOT, BECAUSE WE ASK NOT.

—*F. B. Meyer*

Chapter 7

FINALLY!

I find it interesting to note the fact that when the biblical scholars of the King James Version were putting the book of Acts together, they gave as the heading for it "The Acts of the Apostles." If you've read the book, though, I think you'll agree with me that this is not so much the acts of the apostles as it is the acts of the Holy Spirit. Whenever the apostles performed noteworthy acts, it was actually the Holy Spirit flowing through them. We sometimes credit men and women for what they are doing, when in fact the credit should be given to the Holy Spirit for what He is doing in and through their lives.

We want that same access, that same indwelling of the Holy Spirit, that same manifestation of the Holy Spirit in our lives. However, many people do not understand the difference between emotionalism and the anointing of the Holy Spirit. They might watch one of my church services on television and say that my church members and I are too emotional. I find that most people who express that concern hide behind it because they lack clarity in what it means to have received the anointing of the Spirit. The anointing may evoke emotion, but the reason I am clear that it is not about emotion is that many times my church members and I come into the service and our emotions are completely the opposite of what is demonstrated in the Spirit during our time together. If I operated based on how I felt, there are many times when I would be sitting all scrunched up with my head hanging down, looking pitiful, because that is how I felt at the time. But then I find myself raising my hands, looking up to God, and praising Him in my spirit, because that is how the Holy Spirit feels about it, and the Holy Spirit changes me. It is the anointing of God.

Let us be careful to understand, though, that the anointing is not always about physical expressions or emotions. It is very possible that some people resort to emotionalism and pretend that it is the work of the Holy Spirit, but it will never last. To be under God's anointing is not proven by how loud we get or how high we jump. God's anointing is His empowering that enables us to be effective at what we do. I've seen people teach God's Word and never raise their voice or their hands, and yet they are very effective at what they do. The Holy Spirit is the only one who can make us effective for God.

> *God's anointing is His empowering that enables us to be effective at what we do.*

The Holy Spirit in the Book of Acts

I want to take another look at Acts 2:1–4, as it is at the heart of where I want you to bring you:

> *And when the day of Pentecost was fully come, they were all with one accord in one place. And suddenly there came a sound from heaven as of a rushing mighty wind, and it filled all the house where they were sitting. And there appeared unto them cloven tongues like as of fire, and it sat upon each of them. And they were all filled with the Holy Ghost, and began to speak with other tongues, as the Spirit gave them utterance.*

Something remarkable was going on here. To get everyone in one place, and that they should all be of one accord, is an amazing thing! But God says that when we get in one accord and in one place something good is going to happen! First the house was filled, then the people were filled with the Holy Spirit and enabled to speak with other tongues. From there, the Spirit-filled church in Jerusalem grew by the thousands and began to push outward into the entire civilized world.

I read a recent newspaper article that focused on the decline in spirituality in the United States. According to the article, the number of people who are Christ-centered or God-centered or even religious in any form was down approximately 20 percent. Two exceptions were noted among the interdenominational independent churches and Spirit-filled churches, which were holding their own against the trend to regress and digress. They were holding their own not only numerically but spiritually.

Who should get the credit for these two exceptions to the national trend? I believe that when the Holy Spirit is operating in and flowing through churches, He will draw people. Yes, a Spirit-filled man or woman of God will draw people. But more important than having a Spirit-filled pastor, which is very important, is having a Spirit-filled congregation, because the work of God is in the streets and not in the pews! It is not enough to hear an anointed soloist, or an anointed choir, or an anointed speaker or teacher. We need to move from being spectators to being participants in the raw, infiltrating presence of God that He may indwell our lives in a substantial way.

The good news is that we are all eligible. We don't have to be up on a church stage to be anointed! We don't have to have a great voice to be anointed! We don't have to be able to play beautifully on an instrument to be anointed! On the day of Pentecost, "They were all filled with the Holy Ghost."

I also want to shine a light on Acts 19:1–6. Remember as you read these verses that these were not unbelievers. The Bible calls them disciples who had believed.

> *And it came to pass, that, while Apollos was at Corinth, Paul having passed through the upper coasts came to Ephesus: and finding certain disciples, He said unto them, Have ye received the Holy Ghost since ye believed?*
>
> *And they said unto him, We have not so much as heard whether there be any Holy Ghost.*
>
> *And he said unto them, Unto what then were ye baptized?*
>
> *And they said, Unto John's baptism.*
>
> *Then said Paul, John verily baptized with the baptism of repentance, saying unto the people, that they should believe on him which should come after him, that is, on Christ Jesus. When they heard this, they were baptized in the name of the Lord Jesus. And when Paul had*

*laid his hands upon them, the Holy Ghost came on them;
and they spake with tongues, and prophesied.*

Paul asked these disciples this very important question, "Have you received the Holy Spirit since you believed?" Jot down on a piece of paper or underline these words in your Bible, *received* and *believed*, because this is the premise of all prayer. "Lord, let me receive what I believe!" It suggests that there can be a time differential between believing and receiving, that we can be a believer in Jesus and yet not have received the baptism of the Holy Spirit. When Paul found out their spiritual state, he immediately led them to be baptized in Jesus' name and prayed for them to receive the Holy Spirit.

The experience of these believers is so typical of what I see in most churches today. I am going to use the theme *Finally!* because I think it is so true of most of us in our Christian experience. "I believed . . . *finally*, I received." It was true in my experience, and I trust that *Finally!* will be or was the sentiment of your heart.

> "I believed . . . finally, I received." It was true in my experience, and I trust that Finally! will be or was the sentiment of your heart.

We're going to look deeper into the Holy Spirit's ascension into authority, and we are going to study His journey into intimacy with the believer. This is more than His sitting on the throne in His auspicious reign over this era; this is about us having a personal, intimate, functional relationship with the Holy Spirit. I'm not talking about goose pimples. I used to think that goose pimples were the anointing until I went down and heard Aretha Franklin singing "Respect," and I got 'em again! I said, "This has nothing to do with church!" I saw Tina Turner standing behind a mike with those long legs singing "rollin', rollin', rollin' on the River," and I got chill bumps! I said, "Oh! Got 'em again! This isn't the Holy Spirit either." (I wasn't married then, you know!)

The Holy Spirit is so much more than that! We need to delve into God's Word that we might more fully and deeply understand who we are as believers and what God has already done for us.

We need the Holy Spirit to move in our lives. *Finally!*

Hungry and Thirsty

We have seen that when Jesus came into this world, He was our Emmanuel, "God tabernacled with us." It literally means that He was the dwell-among-us God. As profound as it was to have God dwell among His people, there came a point in the journey when Jesus said, "I have been *with* you, but I shall be *in* you. I am moving from being just the dwell-among-you God to a deeper level of intimacy of being the dwell-in-you God."

Some of us, however, seem to have missed the next level. What I want to dispel is the common Christian ideology that we have one experience with God, which is the sum total of our experience, and we walk away with all that we need. It's a mindset I confront in churches all the time when I bring a message that is intended to feed people, but they're not hungry. They think they have it all. There's nothing less satisfying than preparing a meal for people who feel "full" of themselves; they have it all and aren't interested in the food. Jesus said, "Blessed are they which do hunger and thirst after righteousness: for they shall be filled" (Matthew 5:6). Yet we promote an ideology that suggests to people that they've experienced Christ, so they have it all—they need absolutely nothing, they are complete, it's over—done!

Isn't it ridiculous for us to think that in one moment or from one experience we know all there is to know about God? I've been married to my wife for twenty-eight years, and we're still learning things about each other! How can we then think that we have searched the height, the depth, the breadth, and the width of all that God has for us? We come with our degree in Christianity and our diploma in salvation, then we sit back and relax and never hunger to know God more fully or hold Him more dearly.

> There is a vast difference between knowing Church and knowing God.
> There is a vast difference between knowing the Bible and knowing God.
> It's one thing to know what God said, and it's another to know the One who said it.

The Bible says that Jesus is both "the author and finisher of our faith" (Hebrews 12:2). He wrote it, then He finishes it! We must begin then to understand all that God has prepared for those who seek His face, and it is found in a relationship with the Holy Spirit.

Are we complete in relation to salvation? Absolutely, if our faith is in Jesus Christ. But there is a difference between being a believer bound for heaven and being a receiver of the baptism of the Holy Spirit, which goes beyond salvation into being empowered for service. In order to serve effectively, *we need power.*

The Holy Spirit Brooding

There is a law in theology called the law of first mention. It means that when God introduces or mentions something for the very first time, such as "blood" or "Spirit" or "redemption" or "salvation," He defines the characteristics clearly and succinctly so that we begin to get a pattern that flows throughout the entire Scriptures.

For instance, "In the beginning God created the heaven and the earth" (Genesis 1:1). Here God establishes Himself as the Creator. The creation didn't just happen. As God, He is clearly defining Himself in this manner: "I am the Creator, and I am in charge."

Immediately following that, God tells us for the very first time about the Holy Spirit. "And the earth was without form, and void; and darkness was upon the face of the deep. And the Spirit of God moved upon the face of the waters" (Genesis 1:2). The first thing God tells us about the Holy Spirit is that He "moved." Watch this, because it is very important. "Moved" isn't just the movement of kinetic energy or like when I move my body. The word *move* comes from a Hebrew word that means "to brood." The Holy Spirit brooded over the waters, as a hen broods over her chicks, as a dove over its eggs. The Spirit of God sat on the earth as if to hatch it—there's a brooding process.

The Holy Spirit broods over the raw creation—a lingering, a hatching, a developing. There is something on the earth that God wants to do, and one of the signs that God has a plan for the earth is the brooding of the Holy Spirit. Everything we read after that comes out of the brooding by the Holy Spirit: the bringing forth of the vegetation, the fish of the sea, the fowl of the air, the separation of the firmaments that are above the water from the firmaments that are beneath the waters. It was all there in the raw, but it needed to be hatched, it needed to be developed, it needed to be delivered.

Obviously, God is using anthropomorphic language here. Anthropomorphic terms used in the Bible suggest that God is using things we do understand to explain things we do not understand. He uses human terms to define divine movement. For instance, when it says, "For the eyes of the LORD run to and fro throughout the whole earth, to shew himself strong in the behalf of them whose heart is perfect toward him" (2 Chronicles 16:9), it does not mean that God's eyeballs are running. It means that God is all-knowing, omniscient, but for our sake He defines it as, "I have eyes going

> *He uses something that we do understand to explain something that we don't understand.*

everywhere." We have eyes, and we understand what eyes are. He is letting us know that He sees everything, but because we have nothing that compares to that level of seeing and knowing, He uses something that we do understand to explain something that we don't understand.

Similarly, when it says, "The hand of the LORD was on Elijah" (1 Kings 18:46), it doesn't mean that God was walking around with His hand on Elijah. The Holy Spirit isn't meaning that the Heavenly Father has a body; the Holy Spirit is using our understanding of our own bodies to explain God's work in our lives, which we don't understand. If that were not true, and these statements are literally true, then God is a bird, for David said, "He shall cover thee with his feathers, and under his wings shalt thou trust" (Psalm 91:4).

When we can see something in our mind, it helps us better understand what that something is like. Throughout the Bible, God is described as "a strong tower" or "a consuming fire" or "a mighty rushing wind." Because there are so many things that God does that are incomprehensible, He will use something that we do comprehend to explain something that we do not.

In Genesis 1:2, God is using the imagery of brooding to help us understand the movement of the Holy Spirit. It helps us understand that all that God would hatch, all that God would create, all that God would stir, and all that God would develop is not done instantly, like passing through a drive-through window at McDonald's. With the Holy Spirit, there is lingering, developing, warming, birthing of a relationship in which we stay in the presence of the Lord. And when we linger in His Presence by staying up under His Word, God begins to do things. Thus, when the Holy Spirit works in our lives, this is an expression or symbol of how He does it.

The Holy Spirit as Oil

Another symbol of the Holy Spirit is oil, particularly olive oil and the olive branch. Why? Because the oil is secreted as the olive is bruised. The only way to get the oil out of the olive is to crush the olive. The oil costs the olive its life, its shape and form. The more we bruise and crush the olive, the more oil is secreted. The prophet Isaiah tells us that Jesus "was wounded for our transgressions, he was bruised for our iniquities: the chastisement of our peace was upon him; and with his stripes we are healed" (Isaiah 53:5). Through that bruising we become eligible to receive the oil of the Holy Spirit.

In our own lives, the bruising we have received has brought us to a level of anointing that we could not get any other way. Jesus said it this way, "If we suffer, we shall also reign with him" (2 Timothy 2:12). There is something about suffering that secretes an anointing that cannot be bought, cannot be bottled, cannot be captured—it comes through the bruising of life.

The Holy Spirit as a Dove

The dove is a profound symbol of the Holy Spirit. More than fifty times in Scripture the dove is mentioned. The dove is different from the pigeon, although they are intimately related to each other. The pigeon has a tendency not to migrate, while the dove has a tendency to migrate, moving according to purpose. In the Old Testament, when they would get ready to offer up sacrifices, they would often call for young turtledoves (see Leviticus 5:7). If you recall, Jesus cleared the temple of the Roman vendors who were taking advantage of the Jewish religion and selling offerings at exorbitant prices (see Matthew 21:12). Vendors were selling turtledoves, which were valuable because they had to be captured lest they migrate away in times of scarceness. So the people paid the high prices in order to provide an offering for sacrifice. It is that which eludes us that becomes the most valuable to us. Those things that are common to us become mundane and ritualistic; that which escapes us becomes valuable to us, and we appreciate it because of its elusiveness.

The dove is docile, gentle, and more apt to become a pet in the house than is the pigeon, because a dove has a gentle spirit. The Holy Spirit is a gentle spirit, often referred to as "the Comforter." Jesus said, "And I will pray the Father, and he shall give you another Comforter, that he may abide with you for ever" (John 14:16). He will come and not only rest upon us, but indwell us.

Have you ever been in a church service where the Holy Spirit graciously and gently set down in the service? One of the things that made me hunger for a deeper relationship with the Holy Spirit was those times when I was in a service and without anybody stimulating it or motivating it, there would be a wave of glory sweeping through the church. It wasn't the preaching or the singing, but the Spirit of God would start moving through the congregation in such a way that I knew there was something I couldn't see at work in the midst of the people, and it was different from anything I had experienced before. Did I love the Lord? Absolutely! Had I given my life to the Lord? Absolutely! But my soul hungered to know Him more fully and more dearly through His Spirit.

When Noah was in the ark after the flood deluge had receded, the Bible says he released a dove, and the dove traveled but it came back, having found no rest for the sole of its feet (see Genesis 8:9). Don't just skip over that and think that we are simply talking about doves. We are also looking at the Holy Spirit who visited, fluttered over, and flowed through numerous Old Testament saints. Study from Genesis to Malachi and see the Spirit of God coming upon the prophets, anointing kings and even craftsmen for service, flowing up through the tabernacle of Moses, through the temple of Solomon, and through Zerubbabel's temple. Like a dove in flight searching, searching, searching, it couldn't rest. But go back to Noah's story and note that the second time the dove was dispatched, it came back with an olive branch in its mouth, indicating to Noah it had found a resting place, the floods were abating (see v. 11). The third time the dove was sent out, it returned no more (see v. 12).

I see the literal application of the dove to be symbolic of the journey of the Holy Spirit moving, visiting, and flowing through the Old Testament ceremonies and rituals and prophets and priests and kings, but finding no resting place until there was a man whose name was John who was in the Jordan River baptizing. When John the Baptist looked up and saw Jesus approaching, he declared, "Behold

> *I see the literal application of the dove to be symbolic of the journey of the Holy Spirit moving, visiting, and flowing.*

the Lamb of God, which taketh away the sin of the world" (John 1:29). John the Baptist was the first person recorded as being filled with the Holy Spirit while he was still in his mother's belly (see Luke 1:15). Filled with the Holy Spirit, John knew Jesus not just according to the flesh—though they were cousins—but he knew Him according to the Spirit.

When John went to baptize Jesus, it says, "And Jesus, when he was baptized, went up straightway out of the water: and, lo, the heavens were opened unto him, and he saw the Spirit of God descending like a dove, and lighting upon him: and lo a voice from heaven, saying, This is my beloved Son, in whom I am well pleased" (Matthew 3:16–17). John had called Jesus a sacrifice, "the Lamb of God." God the Father called Jesus His "beloved Son," in whom He was well pleased. And as the Father spoke, look at the dove coming! In case there's any doubt as to the dove, Luke adds to his account, "The Holy Ghost descended in a bodily shape like a dove upon him" (Luke 3:22). God is saying, "This is the resting place of abode for the Holy Spirit."

The Holy Spirit in Jesus' Life

Once the anointing of the Spirit fell upon Jesus, His ministry exploded, indicating He is the Messiah, the Anointed One, and they began to call him Jesus Christ. "Christ" is not His last name. *Christ* means "anointed" and is the Greek translation of the Hebrew word rendered *Messiah*. "Christ" is symbolic of the endowment of the Holy Spirit falling upon Him. It denotes that He was anointed or consecrated to His great redemptive work as Prophet, Priest, and King of the people. He is Jesus *the* Christ. That is why sometimes you will hear Him called "Jesus Christ" and at other times you will hear Him called "Christ Jesus."

When Jesus asked His disciples who men said He was, they suggested John the Baptist or Elijah or Jeremiah. Clearly, they couldn't see "the Christ," only Jesus. But when He asked Peter, Peter answered, "Thou art the Christ, the Son of the living God. And Jesus answered and said unto him, Blessed art thou, Simon Barjona: for flesh and blood hath not re-vealed it unto thee, but my Father which is in heaven" (Matthew 16:16–17). Even Peter could not see this on his own except that God revealed it to him.

Most of the time the disciples only saw Him as Jesus. When they were in the boat and the storm came upon them, Jesus was asleep. Peter came rushing down and cried, "Master, carest thou not that we perish?" (Mark 4:38). What Peter didn't understand was that Jesus might have been asleep, but the Christ never sleeps! There was no reason to get upset then, and there's no reason for us to get upset today when we think God isn't aware of our situation. God never sleeps or slumbers.

So there are some things that we see Jesus do, but we don't see the Christ. The Christ is always there but hidden from view. The glory of God is upon Him and in Him and through Him, yet we see only Jesus Christ. But when He is raised from the dead, we see Him as Christ Jesus. And the Bible says that "the Spirit of him that raised up Jesus from the dead dwell in you, he that raised up Christ from the dead shall also quicken your mortal bodies by his Spirit that dwelleth in you" (Romans 8:11). If you don't give a shout at that thought, you better think about it again!

God wants us to realize that He has more for us than just dressing up and coming to church. He has more for us than going through a routine and a form of religion. What He has always wanted was a relationship with us. In the Garden of Eden, God had set Adam in a place of relationship from which sin drove him out. Man's relationship with God was broken but patched through the blood of bullocks and goats, patched at the tabernacle, and patched at the temple. But it wasn't fixed until Jesus went to the Cross and died for our sins. "It is finished" declared that we were once again connected with God.

Now watch this! When we look at salvation, we see the "re" prefix before it—redeemed, restored, revived, renewed—because Christ came to succeed where Adam failed at bridging the gap that we might be reconnected to a place of intimacy with God. How intimate was this that He left His royal throne of glory, the host of heaven, and the royal diadem and stepped down through forty-two generations, came down to the dressing room of a virgin named Mary, wrapped Himself up in flesh, that He might become a Kinsman Redeemer and become kin to us and dwell among us.

The dwell-among-us God walked past blind Bartimaeus, who sat by the highway begging, and through that close association the blinded eyes were opened that he might receive his sight. The woman with the issue of blood who got close enough to touch the garment hem of the dwell-among-us God was healed and delivered of her illness. Lazarus was in the grave decomposing, stinking, and falling apart. The dwell-among-us God never even laid a hand on Lazarus. He simply said, "Lazarus, come forth!" and the putrefaction stopped, the decaying flesh waxed warm, the blood started liquefying, the heart started pumping, the lungs started breathing, and the tissues began receiving oxygen. Lazarus rose and began thumping his way out of the grave, just because the dwell-among-us God was near.

Now, however, the dwell-among-us God says, "I have been with you, but I shall be in you!" *Finally!* "We who were afar off have been drawn nigh." *Finally*, we are reconnected! *Finally*, we are restored to a place of intimacy! *Finally!*

Finally Pentecost

In reality, man has been waiting for the experience of Pentecost since the fall of man, through the flying of the doves, through the offerings of the scapegoats, through the burning of the lambs, and the sprinkling of the blood. Man has been waiting, substituting shadows; for in the absence of the reality, the shadow had to make do. But when that which is perfect was come, all of a sudden we don't have to slay the lamb anymore, we don't have to put blood on the doors, someone has taken the place of the lamb; He is the great I AM!

Now you see why Acts 2:1 says, "When the day of Pentecost was *fully come*." *Finally!* "When the day of Pentecost was fully come" was a journey. And then, *"Suddenly* there came a sound from heaven as of a rushing mighty wind!" After waiting all this time for that for which we believed to receive it, after waiting for ages and ages for that which God had in store to come, once they got in one place and in one accord, *suddenly!* Just because we have been waiting a long time for God to do something in our lives doesn't mean we can't have a *"suddenly"* experience with God. They tarried in the Old Testament because they were waiting for the Holy Spirit to set up His inaugural position in the earth. We don't have to tarry anymore. We are not waiting on God; now God is waiting on us!

> *We are not waiting on God; now God is waiting on us!*

Jesus said to His disciples before His ascension into heaven, "Ye shall receive power, after that the Holy Ghost is come upon you: and ye shall be witnesses unto me both in Jerusalem, and in all Judaea, and in Samaria, and unto the uttermost part of the earth" (Acts 1:8). The disciples had been eyewitnesses to the resurrected Christ. They had taken His dead body down off the Cross and prepared it for burial. They were in the upper room when Jesus came to them there. They had felt the nail holes in His hands and seen the wound in His side. And yet the Bible says "ye shall be witnesses." I thought they already were witnesses! Nobody could have been more of an eyewitness than any of the disciples. And yet He said they were not witnesses, but they would be witnesses after the Holy Spirit has come upon them.

Christ is not just talking about witnessing the resurrection. He's talking about witnessing the blood hitting the mercy seat! The Holy Spirit was the only one who could bear witness that Jesus' blood had hit the heavenly mercy seat and that our sins had been remitted, so the Gospel could be preached and lived with power. Thus Jesus told them to stay in Jerusalem and not preach anything until the Holy Spirit came upon them.

Years ago, when they first came out with the big satellite dishes, I got one. At the time, I had a two-bedroom house with a 5' x 8' kitchen and a 9' x 12' living room and an almost

10' dish in the backyard. The dish was almost as big as the house! I needed that big dish so I could receive the satellite waves that were already in the air. Once I had a receiver, all kinds of stations that had been there all the time were now accessible to me. What I'm trying to get you to understand is that God has some stuff for you that you have been missing, but after that the Holy Spirit comes upon you, you will receive the power!

When the disciples were filled with the Holy Spirit in Acts 2, they began to speak in languages that they had not learned. They spoke, and God gave the language. Most of us misunderstand the dynamic at work here. There was a time when I'd see people dance in the Spirit, but I couldn't do it. I guess I was waiting for God to grab my foot. I remember praying, "God, I want to praise You in the Spirit, but I can't do it. What is wrong with You, Lord, that You won't give me a dance?" I didn't understand that a dance was something I give to Him. I thought the Holy Spirit would make me praise God. I discovered He anoints us to praise Him.

Let me show you that even though the anointing is there, you have control of the switch. There have been times when I was in the grocery store and started to think about something that God had done in my life, and I got so filled with the

Spirit I could have danced. The apostle Paul said, "The spirits of the prophets are subject to the prophets" (1 Corinthians 14:32). Paul says that through the act of our will we have an option in

> *Even though the anointing is there, you have control of the switch.*

how we operate. He states, "I will pray with the spirit, and I will pray with the understanding also: I will sing with the spirit, and I will sing with the understanding also" (1 Corinthians 14:15). That means, contrary to what anyone else may tell you, praying in the spirit is not about understanding. That is a hard statement for people who are used to understanding and intellectualizing everything.

But understand that as long as we approach God on a strictly intellectual level, God can be no bigger than our minds. We have incarcerated Him within the limitations of our intellects. However, God cannot be held there. He said, "For as the heavens are higher than the earth, so are my ways higher than your ways, and my thoughts than your thoughts" (Isaiah 55:9). The apostle Paul says I have another option: I can receive on two levels—I can pray in the Spirit, and I can pray with understanding also.

What happened in Acts 2 happened again in

Acts 10:44–45: "While Peter yet spake these words, the Holy Ghost fell on all them which heard the word. And they of the circumcision which believed were astonished, as many as came with Peter, because that on the Gentiles also was poured out the gift of the Holy Ghost." This was the first outpouring of the Holy Spirit on the Gentiles. Despite all that God had done by His Spirit, the Jewish believers ("the circumcised") did not want to believe that a nasty, dirty, perverse Gentile centurion from Rome and his household and other Gentile friends could receive the Holy Spirit. Remember, the Jews were so against the Gentiles that if a Gentile ate with them, they would break the plate. It's easy to see why they were "astonished" that the Gentiles were filled with the Holy Spirit. What convinced them it was for real? "For they heard them speak with tongues, and magnify God. Then answered Peter, Can any man forbid water, that these should not be baptized, which have received the Holy Ghost as well as we?" (vv. 46–47).

Nearly ten years after this event, and almost twenty years after the day of Pentecost, Paul found the group of disciples in Ephesus who had not received the Holy Spirit since they believed (Acts 19:1–6). They had never even heard of the Holy Spirit. Although the gift of the Holy Spirit was there for them, they couldn't receive what they didn't know was theirs. But as soon as they heard about it, they could and did receive it. Much like the satellite signals in the air, the gift of the Spirit had been there all along, but they did not have the receiver until Paul showed them the way.

Be Filled with the Spirit

Here's a truth you do not want to miss. "Eye hath not seen, nor ear heard, neither have entered into the heart of man, the things which God hath prepared for them that love him. But God hath revealed them unto us by his Spirit: for the Spirit searcheth all things, yea, the deep things of God" (1 Corinthians 2:9–10). When you get into God's Spirit, you can get what God has for you.

I'm going to show you one more thing. When I was living in sin, I was empty; and many of the nasty, dirty sinful things that I did occurred *because* I was empty. In the absence of many things to dwell in me, whatever was around me filled my space. Truth be told, an empty glass is really not empty—it is filled with

> *When I was living in sin, I was empty; and many of the nasty, dirty sinful things that I did occurred because I was empty.*

air. The reason there is air in the otherwise empty glass is that it is vulnerable to that which is around it. It's the same with us. In the absence of anything else, whatever is around us will fill our space.

When I came to Jesus, He came into my heart, much like the water poured from a pitcher fills an "empty" glass, and He lives in me. Now, this is where Pentecostal people confused me, because they tried to tell me that I did not have the Spirit, and I knew that wasn't true. I knew that I had tasted and seen that the Lord is good (Psalm 34:8). I knew that Jesus was in me by His Spirit.

However, I didn't know the difference between having the Spirit and being filled with the Spirit. Jesus said, "The water that I shall give him shall be in him a well of water springing up into everlasting life" (John 4:14). Jesus had to be in me before He could spring up in me. I couldn't get the Holy Ghost to spring up in my life if He wasn't in my life.

Jesus also said, "If any man thirst, let him come unto me, and drink. He that believeth on me, as the scripture hath said, out of his belly shall flow rivers of living water. (But this spake he of the Spirit, which they that believe on him should receive: for the Holy Ghost was not yet given; because that Jesus was not yet glorified)" (John 7:37–39). That day has passed—the Holy Spirit has been given, and it's time for the living water to flow through us.

Imagine that I have a pitcher filled with water, which represents the Holy Spirit, and I have a glass with some water in it, which represents me. If I pour more water in the glass, I have more glory. If I keep filling the glass, the water that is in the inside will start to overflow on the outside, pouring over the sides of the glass onto the floor. This is what it is to be filled with the Holy Ghost until what is on the inside starts flowing onto the outside!

God wants your cup to overflow with His presence! So stand up, open your mouth, and give God the praise! When you praise Him from your heart, He will fill you up! If you forget about yourself, come out of your pride, and stop worrying about what you heard or what you thought, then out of your belly will flow rivers of living waters! Praise Him! Praise Him! Praise Him! Praise Him! Praise Him! And don't stop.

If you always do what you've always done, you'll always get what you've always gotten. This is your time to get a supernatural gully-washing, thirst-quenching, mind-renewing touch from the living God! It's real! It's not just a Pentecostal thing; it's not just a Methodist thing; it's not just a Presbyterian thing; it's a Jesus thing!

God wants to fill you with the Holy Ghost until you speak in tongues as the Spirit gives you utterance. He wants your cup to overflow! He wants to meet your need! He wants to quench your thirst! God has something for you! God has a blessing for you! Reach out and grab it! You've got to have it! Open your mouth and praise the Lord!

Come out of your tradition.
Come out of your guilt.
Come out of your shame.
Come out of your condemnation.
Come out of your past.
Come out of your weakness.

Praise Him until you come all the way out!
Praise Him until your soul is free!
Praise Him until you see the doubt fly away!
Praise Him until the heavenly dove falls!
Praise Him until the water gushes!

Throw your hands up and say, "I want it!
I'm tired of religion! I'm tired of playing games!
Fill my cup!"

He who hungers and thirsts shall be filled.
Come and be filled!
Receive the Holy Ghost.
He is yours!